Reason and Prediction

Reason and Prediction

Simon Blackburn

Fellow of Pembroke College, Oxford

Cambridge
at the University Press
1973

Published by the Syndics of the Cambridge University Press
Bentley House, 200 Euston Road, London NW1 2DB
American Branch: 32 East 57th Street, New York, N.Y. 10022

© Cambridge University Press 1973

Library of Congress Catalogue Card Number: 72-83580

ISBN: 0 521 087422

Printed in Great Britain by
Western Printing Services Ltd
Bristol

Contents

Preface

This book originated as a Ph.D. thesis, which was submitted to the University of Cambridge in 1969, and examined by Sir Alfred Ayer and Dr Mary Hesse. The opportunity to do much of the work which led to it was created by a Research Fellowship which I held at Churchill College for the preceding two years.

I would like to thank many friends at Cambridge and Oxford, particularly E. J. Craig and J. J. Altham, for much discussion and constant interest. Most of all I would like to express my debt to Dr C. Lewy, without whose patience and encouragement nothing would have been done.

Oxford, April 1972   S.W.B.

To the Memory of Timothy Blackburn

Introduction

The subject of this book is a certain way of reasoning. This way of reasoning provides the basis for some of our most familiar expectations and beliefs: it is not the property of the scientist or of the statistician, but of all of us. The experience of every one of us is limited and fragmentary, for we each perceive only a little of the world, as it now is, and remember only a fraction of the world as it once was. Yet the scope of our beliefs is wider than this. We award ourselves the right to believe a great variety of things whose truth is in no way a matter of our experience: we believe things about other people's minds, or about the meaning of their words, or about the existence of physical objects independent of ourselves, or about what is good or bad. Most of the central problems of philosophy grow from the realisation that confidence in a belief of one of these kinds can appear insecure or even indefensible. My topic is simply belief which we have because we expect uniformities in our experience to be representative. They will, we think, display themselves on occasions of which we have no experience, and so we award ourselves the right to believe that at least in some respects the future should resemble the past, and the unobserved should resemble the observed. Corresponding to this belief is a way of reasoning, which we use when we suppose that something will be so, because it has been so, or that something outside our experience should possess some feature, because similar things within our experience possess it. The utility of such reasoning is evident, for it is the basis of the very first steps beyond the fragmentary beliefs which perception can guarantee. But its insecurity is almost as evident. Whether it is defensible is the question to which this book is addressed. It is a question which can take the title of the problem of induction.

The mode of reasoning that I have described is not a very popular topic with contemporary analytic philosophers, at least in Britain, and the causes of this are manifold. Partly there is despair that in spite of its magnificent history, the problem has not been settled. Partly there is fashion, and partly there are things still more disreputable. One such cause of neglect is the feeling that the problem only arises in specialist philosophy of science, because the mode of reasoning which is its subject is peculiar to scientists. It should be evident already that this is utterly wrong: the belief that my typewriter will not suddenly become weightless, change colour, or talk to me, is not the result of scientific investigation. It is to be justified, if at all, by reasoning common to all men. Another cause of neglect is fear that the matter is too technical and best left to confirmation theorists, probability theorists or even statisticians. But the problem is not a technical one, and exactly as in other branches of philosophy we require only that understanding of neighbouring disciplines which is necessary to estimate the extent, if any, of their contributions.

A third cause of neglect will introduce the course which the book takes. After the failure of many attempts to show inductive reasoning to be defensible, philosophers naturally came to be suspicious of the problem. Perhaps, it was felt, a proper view of the notions involved in framing the problem would reveal that a particular sort of knowledge is indeed a reason for a belief about the future, or about things which we have not observed. We could hope to reveal this by paying sufficient attention to the meanings of the words used, particularly the word "reason". But then, the best way of identifying the notion of a reason seems to be to look at the way in which we do reason, and once we think this it can easily appear as though there could be no proper activity of criticising the ways of reasoning we adopt, for these just define what we take the term "reason" to mean. It would be like criticising us for taking the word "elephant" to refer to a particular sort of large animal. In something like this way, the feeling that inductive reasoning needs a defence came to be stifled.

This argument, which can also be deployed in other areas of philosophy, recalls Bertrand Russell's remark about the advantages of theft over honest toil. But it can only be finally laid when we have a superior account of the concept of a reason and of our purposes in reasoning, which makes it clear whether there is a problem of defending inductive reasoning, and if so, what sort of problem that is. The book therefore starts with an investigation of the concept of a reason. We find, broadly, that since we demand something of a process of reasoning, namely that it should be reliable, there is a problem of showing that any particular form of reasoning meets that demand. The truth of the evidence must be reliably connected with the truth of the conclusion. This demand, described in detail, has consequences in other parts of philosophy. For example, it is not uncommon for writers on the philosophy of mind to postulate a basic right to use things that we can observe as a reason for conclusions concerning other people's mental states. But we can only rely on such a right if we have an account of the truth conditions of the evidence and of the conclusion which enables us to depend upon them being true together – a point which Wittgenstein appears to have apprehended more clearly than some of his followers.

The chapters which seek to establish the nature of the problem are doing what is sometimes described as conceptual analysis. That is, they are concerned with arriving at a better understanding of a concept which is pervasive in our thinking: the concept of a reason. To do this they perforce make claims about whether one thing means the same as another, or whether to say one thing is just to say this other thing, or whether one proposition is identical with another. Some philosophers find such notions problematical, because it is so difficult to give a general account of what has to be true for two things to be synonymous. This is quite right, but we do not have to analyse everything before we start to say anything, and in fact the use I make of the notions puts no undue strain on the notion of meaning. It is exactly like discussing whether one person is identical with another, which can be done even although our understanding of personal identity is only partial. Other philosophers might claim that the very idea of one thing meaning the same as another is unintelligible, but few philosophers believe that this is true, and fewer still practise as though it were true. Doubtful arguments in the theory of meaning exact too high a price when they ask us to classify as unintelligible some of the greatest achievements of, say, Plato, Hume, Frege and Russell.

Once the concept of a reason is identified sufficiently closely for us to know what would count as a defence of a particular type of reasoning, the work switches its attention to the sort of resemblance which we expect the unobserved to bear to the observed. This needs to be done because it is not at all obvious how to describe just which resemblances we expect to obtain, and what the basis for this selection is. Thus there exists argument that it is simply because of the history of the language that we expect the sky to be blue tomorrow rather than red. This is a very depressing thought, because if it is true it would seem to be just the result of a historical accident that we count one belief as more reasonable than the other. Fortunately this view can be shown to be false, but when that is done other features of the resemblances for which we reason come to light. For example, it emerges that most formal work in probability theory or confirmation theory is bound to be insufficient to lead to a defence of inductive reasoning.

This mightn't matter, except that someone who thinks inductive reasoning to be indefensible will naturally take comfort in the difficulty of showing its conclusions to be at all probable. So I enter on a discussion of the way in which the concept of probability is one which it is preferable to avoid, because it has features which suit a sceptic's purposes too well. The point here is that we must beware of the common equation of defending a form of reasoning with showing its conclusions to be probable. For probabilities are things of which we can easily be regarded as ignorant, and this would then translate into inability to show that our form of reasoning is a good one.

If we avoid this pitfall, we may try to defend our form of reasoning by drawing out its general connection with success in prediction. This is the matter of the last three chapters. The work here depends heavily on a proper handling of the notorious principle of indifference. This is the principle which, for example, entitles one to be more cheerful if lost on a mountain where most directions lead to safety than if lost on one where most directions do not. I argue that a great deal of our reasoning needs the principle, and in spite of its infamous reputation it may have close links with the very notion of a reason. The final chapters concentrate upon the possibility that certain ways of reasoning must, in general, give us the truth, and therefore possess all the security that we need. Particularly perhaps they must give us the truth if we live in a world of independent objects, and I try to fortify this idea in the final chapter. There is much in these regions which is largely unexplored, and this is a pity because, whether or not it follows quite my path, it seems that any defence of inductive reasoning will have to pass through them.

I

A statement of the problem

What is to be justified?

We often use one proposition as a reason for another. Sometimes each proposition has the same subject, but each predicates a different thing of it. For example, we may use the proposition that a certain person is stupid as a reason for the proposition that he ought not to be made a general. Or the proposition that he is groaning may be used as a reason for believing that he is in pain. It requires little reflection to see that in each case we could raise the question of why we are right to reason like this. And the answer, if one is to be had, would come by relating the two attributes predicated in some way: in the first case this is a task for moral philosophy, and in the second case for the philosophy of mind. But the attributes involved may bear a closer relation to each other than in these examples. We might use the proposition that a certain thing is twenty years old as a reason for the proposition that it is over ten years old, and we would certainly be right to do this, for the second proposition follows from the first, and we can see that it does (much later I shall discuss what happens if one proposition follows from another but we *can't* see that it does). But we shall not be much concerned with cases where the conclusion follows from the evidence. Finally, the two propositions may attribute the same thing to the same subject, but at different times. So we may use the proposition that the rug we see is red now as a reason for believing that it will be red in five minutes' time, or for believing that it was red before we entered the room. Or, we may use the proposition that it was red as a reason for believing that it is still red. In each case we use the proposition that a thing has or had some property as a reason for the proposition that it has, will have, or had the same property at some different time – or, more ambitiously, at all different times. Trivial cases exist in which the evidence entails the conclusion: we can use the proposition that a person is an orphan or a graduate now as a reason for supposing that he will be so tomorrow. But there are other cases where although the evidence is true the conclusion could be false, for the thing could have changed or could in the future change in the respect in question, and it is these cases which are our concern. Part of the problem to which this book is addressed is the nature and justification of such reasoning.

There are other expectations of similarity, for so far we have only mentioned cases where the propositions concern the same thing. But we often use the proposition that something is true of some things of a certain kind as a reason for the proposition that it is true of some other, or all other, things of that kind. Having discovered that a number of slugs eat cabbages I might use this as a reason for supposing that this slug that I have just found eats cabbages, or even for supposing that all slugs eat cabbages. There need not always be a distinction between the expectation that a particular thing will remain the same, and the expectation that some things of a sort are like other things of that sort. For example, the expectation that this spot of ground will continue for the next twenty-four hours to be, as it always has been, one which the sun begins to illuminate at twenty-four-hour intervals is the same thing as the expectation that today's event of the sun rising will, like its predecessors, be followed in twenty-four hours by a similar event. Yet the first is cast in the form of an expectation that a thing remains the same, and the second in the form of an expectation that one thing (event) of a sort will be like others of the same sort. Nevertheless, the distinction is a convenient one to make, for not all expectations of one form translate into expectations of the other form.

It is the reasoning that I have described, the use of certain sorts of evidence as a reason for certain related propositions, that is the subject of his book. If we call the proposition that we use as a reason for another the I-evidence (without, of course, prejudging the question whether it is ever good evidence) and the proposition for which we are reasoning the I-conclusion, then we can collect together the things I have said like this. I-propositions divide into two sorts. Sometimes an I-proposition asserts that some thing a had a feature F at some time, or that it will be F at some time, or that it is F now, or is F at all times, where it is contingent that a is F. In this case I-evidence is that the thing a was F at some other times than those mentioned in the I-conclusion, and this evidence does not entail the conclusion. In the other sort of case an I-proposition asserts that some, or all, things of a kind A are F, where it is contingent that if anything is A it is F. In this case I-evidence is that some other thing or things of kind A are F.

The questions to which we are to give a solution are whether, and why, we are ever right to use I-evidence as a reason for an I-conclusion. These are the problems of the clarification, and the justification, of induction.

There is a notable feature of I-propositions. An I-proposition need not be a generalisation, that is, a universally qualified hypothesis. It may simply assert that some other As are F, not that *all* others are, or that an object a will be F at some time, not at *all* times. Now this is not a drawback; on the contrary, there are clearly cases in which we give reasons for predictions which are not as strong as generalisations. Given that I have failed to mend bicycle punctures on all of a number of attempts I am prepared to predict that I shall fail on this occasion, but not really interested in whether I shall always fail. But certain authors have thought that reasoning for generalisations is fundamental. Von Wright for example has an argument designed to show that particular I-propositions cannot be reasonably believed unless some generalisation is reasonably believed. Now if this is a good argument it clearly alters the character of the enquiry, for it would mean that we need only consider generalisations and reasoning for them to begin with, resting assured that until we can justify this reasoning no particular I-proposition will be justifiable either. Von Wright considers what could be a reason for the hesitation to generalise:

"... we entertain a suspicion that some feature (or features) C, *other* than A, is to be held 'responsible' for the fact that all A's so far observed have been B. If C is present in an A, then this A will be B. But if C is absent from an A, B *may* be absent too. Thus the eduction that the next A will be B gets its 'legitimacy' from our belief in a general proposition to the effect that all A's which are C are also B *and* our belief that this C, whatever it may be, will accompany the next A."[1]

This is Von Wright's argument for supposing that the use of eduction, that is, reasoning for I-propositions which are not generalisations, is logically secondary to reasoning for generalisation. But it fails, because it confuses the following two things:

[1] Von Wright, *The Logical Problem of Induction*, 1957, p. 11.

(a)   We entertain a suspicion, of some particular feature (features) *C* other than *A*, that it is (they are) to be held responsible for the the fact that all *A*s so far observed have been *B*.

(b)   We entertain a suspicion that there exists some feature (features) *C* other than *A*, which is (are) to be held responsible for the fact that all *A*s so far observed have been *B*.

Now it may well be the case that whenever we believe that some *A*s are *B* but not that all *A*s are *B*, we believe that there exists some feature differentiating those *A*s that are *B* from those that are not. So in any such case (b) may well be true. But Von Wright needs (a) to be true: only (a) can show that it is not reasonable to believe the particular proposition without its being reasonable to believe some generalisation. For if (b) is true we only believe that some feature *C* exists such that all *CA*s are *B*, and this is not believing a generalisation, it is only believing that there *exists* some true generalisation. But there is no reason for supposing that instead (a) is true whenever we have confidence that a particular I-proposition is true, but do not have confidence that the generalisation is true. For there is a world of difference between believing that there is some feature responsible for a regularity in our experience, and believing that we have found what it is. If the latter were always true when we hesitate to generalise, science would be much easier. So Von Wright needs to show that every case of eduction without inductive generalisation depends upon belief in some other generalisation. But his argument for this depends upon the confusion between 'There is a proposition of the form that all *CA*s are *B* which we believe to be true' and 'We believe that there exists some proposition of the form that all *CA*s are *B* which is true.' That the latter and not the former is true in cases of rational hesitation to generalise does not show that rational belief in particular I-propositions depends upon rational belief in some universally quantified ones, nor that reasoning for particular I-propositions is in any way secondary to reasoning for universally quantified ones.

But there may be other arguments for this conclusion. Strawson thinks that acceptance of any inductive argument as "sound or correct or reasonable" is the same as acceptance of a generalisation, even if the inductive argument does not have a generalisation as conclusion. He thinks however that it would be misleading to restrict consideration to the support of generalisations because these "do not often appear in practice" as the conclusions of arguments from particular instances. He views them as suppressed premisses, themselves contingent, which if added would make the argument deductively valid. Thus discussing the argument which he calls (b): 'The kettle's been on the fire for the last ten minutes, so it should be boiling by now', he says:

> "Thus our acceptance of the non-necessary proposition that all kettles boil within ten minutes of being put on the fire will be the same as our acceptance of the non-deductive principle that the fact that a kettle has been on the fire for ten minutes is a good ground for concluding that it will be boiling; and both are the same as our acceptance of the step in (b) as sound or correct or reasonable."[2]

Clearly if this is accepted we can again restrict our attention to reasoning for universally quantified hypotheses, since the acceptance of any other non-deductive argument as sound or correct or reasonable will be the same as acceptance of one of these as true; namely that one which added to the premiss makes the inference deductively valid. So the view is that we should accept that P is a good ground or reason for Q if and only if we believe some universal hypothesis R, such that P and R together entail Q. But this is by no means obvious. One would normally accept 'big black clouds are looming up' as a reason for expecting it to rain without accepting the generalisation 'whenever big black clouds loom up it rains'. Indeed this proposition is most unlikely: all one would believe is 'in most cases, when big black clouds loom up, it rains'. But this no longer suffices to give us a parallel deductive form of the reasoning. Nor is there any universally quantified hypothesis which both looks likely and can be added to 'big black clouds are looming up and in most cases when big black clouds loom up it rains' to give a deductively valid argument to the conclusion that it will rain. If we tried we should need some hypothesis of the form 'whenever both these premisses are true it rains', and this is equivalent again to saying that in all, and not merely most, cases when big black clouds loom up it rains. So Strawson fails to show that to put the enquiry in terms of justification of general propositions which function as suppressed premisses is "merely to put the general problem in a more specific, and less realistic, form" (p. 236). In

---

[2] Strawson, *Introduction to Logical Theory*, 1963, p. 236.

fairness it should be added that he goes on to give an account of certain examples (pp. 239, 240) which does not depend upon this view, and, indeed, contradicts it. For there he agrees that a good argument might exist although the most ambitious general proposition we should accept would just state that something is true in most cases, and so, as I have described, fail to yield a parallel deductively valid argument.

I shall discuss in detail the relation between 'P is a reason for Q', and 'in most cases, when P is true, Q is true' later (ch. 6). For the present all that we need to notice is that it is most implausible to suppose that in order to believe 'P is a reason for Q' we need to believe any universally quantified hypothesis connecting P with Q. Again, there is no reason to shift the enquiry entirely to reasoning for universal hypotheses.

It is of course easy to see how concern with scientific theories and laws should lead philosophers to concentrate upon the support of general hypotheses. But not all I-propositions are generalisations, and as we have been it is not clear that the problem of reasons for generalisations in any way underlies the problem of reasons for those that are not.

Suppose we now ask what exactly it is that we might be asked to justify. It seems at first sight as though there are two different answers. We might be asked to justify ever believing an I-proposition if we have only I-evidence for it. Or, we might be asked to justify ever taking I-evidence as a reason for an I-proposition. These certainly seem to be different problems. A parallel difference arises in considering the probability of propositions, for showing that a conclusion is probable is a very different matter from showing that some evidence which we have raises its probability. I shall consider the relation between these two problems in detail when we have an account of what it is for one proposition to be a reason for another, and of what it is for a belief to be reasonable.

At present I shall consider only the second request, the request to justify our ever taking I-evidence as a reason for an I-proposition. Without being unduly linguistic or analytic it is natural to expect that the nature and difficulty of this request can only be grasped when we have a working idea of the concept of a reason, and of its purpose and of its logic. To demonstrate the importance that attaches to a correct understanding of the concept of a reason here

I shall start by considering one answer to the problem, that of Paul Edwards.[3]

The dissolution of the problem

Edwards discusses the justification of induction in the slightly, but here unimportantly, different terms of whether positive instances of a phenomenon provide a reason for supposing unobserved instances to be positive. He claims that it is *analytic* that this is so. He further claims that this being so any philosopher who apparently denies that these things are reasons, must covertly be using the word "reason" in a different sense from that normally given to it. This does not follow from the analyticity claim, for it is consistent with that claim to suppose that people who apparently deny that observed positive instances of a phenomenon provide a reason for supposing unobserved instances to be positive, really are denying this, and are thereby denying an analytic proposition. But at any rate, Edwards thinks that people apparently denying this are either misusing the word "reason", or denying an analytic proposition. The parallel with somebody's misuse of the word "reason" which he gives is that of someone who apparently denies that there are several thousand physicians in New York. But it turns out that this person is using the word "physician" to mean 'person with a medical degree who can cure any conceivable illness in less than two minutes', and, using the word "physician" to mean this, what is then expressed by the sentence "There are several thousand physicians in New York" is false. But equally obviously, somebody using the word in this sense is not denying what we assert when we say that there are several thousand physicians in New York. Edwards considers a philosophical sceptic to be in just this position with regard to the word "reason".

> "So far as I can see, there are three different trends in the ordinary usage of 'reason for an inductive conclusion' . . . one is much more prominent than the others. It may fitly be called the main sense of the word. According to this main sense what we mean when we claim that we have a reason for a prediction is that the past observations of this phenomenon or

[3] Edwards, "Bertrand Russell's Doubts about Induction", reprinted in *Logic and Language*, 1st Series, ed. Flew, 1951.

of analogical phenomena are of a certain kind: they are exclusively or predominantly positive, the number of positive observations is at least fairly large, and they come from extensively varied sets of circumstances . . . It should now be clear that when Russell says that observed instances are never by themselves a reason for an inductive conclusion, he is guilty of *ignoratio elenchi* by redefinition."[4]

According to Edwards, he is meaning by "reason", logically conclusive reason. It should in passing be pointed out that it is extremely unlikely that Russell did mean by "reason", logically conclusive reason, in view of his statement, in the chapter to which Edwards refers, that: "We have not to seek for a proof that [our expectations] *must* be fulfilled but only for some reason in favour of the view that they are *likely* to be fulfilled."[5] But what is important in this passage from Edwards is his account of the main sense of "having a reason for a prediction", and the corresponding "dissolution" of the problem of induction in the form in which I have presented it. For clearly if his account of the concept of reason is correct, there is no question of justifying our use of I-evidence as a reason for an I-proposition, any more than there is a question of justifying taking bachelors to be unmarried males.

There are, I think, three main lines of attack on this sort of approach to the problem of induction, and I shall develop two of them here. The first, which I shall fully discuss in a later chapter,[6] is that for anything like this approach to be correct some considerable restriction has to be put upon the notion of an 'instance of a phenomenon'. For in fact something may be observed to be true of all of a wide variety of things of a certain sort, and yet give no reason for supposing it to be true of certain unobserved things of that sort. At present this must be taken upon trust, but a full discussion of it will be given when I consider Goodman's paradox. However, this does not uncover Edwards's fundamental mistakes. For in the face of this sort of objection he could apparently restate his position in terms of those restricted types of instance of restricted types of phenomenon in which inductive evidence *does* provide a reason

---

[4] Edwards, p. 67.

[5] Russell, *The Problems of Philosophy*, 1962 (1st edn 1912), p. 62. Russell's italics.

[6] Chapter 4.

for a prediction, and claim that when this is so it is analytic that it is so, and the sceptic still guilty of *ignoratio elenchi*.

The second objection is to the principal contention of his article, the claim that we are just asserting, when we say that we have a reason for an inductive conclusion, that we have knowledge of certain positive instances. For there are excellent grounds for denying Edwards's analyticity claim, and its consequence that anybody who is apparently sceptical about I-evidence being a reason for an I-conclusion is either denying an analytic proposition, or misusing the word "reason". However, we must distinguish Edwards's claim from something with which it may easily be confused. There are philosophers who think it an empirical fact that it is rational to use inductive procedures; they think that because these procedures have proved successful in the past it is reasonable to use them now, that this is contingent, and if they had not proved successful it would not be reasonable to use them now. Again there are philosophers who think that it is an empirical fact that inductive procedures are rational, because their being so is contingent upon certain very general facts being true of the world. On the other hand there are some philosophers who have thought it logically necessary that inductive evidence provides a reason for belief, and have thought that this could be established by some sort of conceptual investigation alone. It seems to me quite possible that this last group is right, but they are not saying just what Edwards is saying. For, without attempting to consider the difference between logically necessary propositions and the sub-class of analytic propositions, I think it should be clear that it is an open question whether or not it is provable by conceptual means alone that some inductive evidence is a reason for belief in some I-propositions, even although "reason for an I-proposition" does not just *mean* 'positive past observations of the same phenomenon', even although to say that someone's belief in such a proposition was reasonable is not *just* to say that he knows that past instances drawn from a wide variety of circumstances were predominantly positive. So, in rebutting Edwards's analyticity claim, we are leaving it open whether giving I-evidence as a reason for an I-conclusion is necessarily or contingently a correct thing to do. But is Edwards's analysis of what it is to give a reason for an I-proposition correct?

The first point to mention is, I think, fairly obvious. Let us suppose that I-evidence is used to provide a reason for an I-proposition;

it does not follow from this alone that it is analytic that it does so, or that anybody denying that it does so is contradicting himself, or using the word "reason" in a peculiar sense. The fact that we use such evidence as a reason does not by itself establish whether it is contingent, or logically necessary, or analytic, or even true, that it is a reason. To take what I shall later argue to be a very close parallel, the fact that we all use an action's producing pain as a reason for supposing that it is wrong does not by itself establish that it is analytic that this feature is a reason for supposing it wrong, either in virtue of some fact about the concept of reason or that of wrongness. The fact that we use I-evidence as a reason for I-propositions is quite consistent with the supposition that we do so because of some other belief about that evidence, such as the belief that it raises the probability of the I-proposition, or even makes it certain that it is true. It follows that simply pointing out that we do use such evidence is not sufficient to establish the analyticity claim. This may easily be obscured by misapplication of the "meaning = use" thesis. Consider the following argument:

(a) Meaning = use.
(b) I-evidence is used as a reason for an I-proposition.
(c) The use of the word "reason" is such that I-evidence provides a reason for an I-proposition.
(d) The meaning of the word "reason" is such that I-evidence provides a reason for an I-proposition.
(e) It is analytic (cannot be doubted without self-contradiction, or convicting oneself of not knowing the meaning of "reason" or some other term) that I-evidence provides a reason for an I-proposition.

This argument does not appear explicitly in Edwards's paper, but it seems to me to be the most plausible version of something which is implicit in his approach. Consider for example the assertion following his account of the senses of "reason": "Anybody who takes the trouble to observe the ordinary usage of the word 'reason' in connection with inductive arguments can easily check up on these claims."[7] What we can easily observe is that I-evidence is used as a reason for an I-conclusion, so may allow ourselves premiss (b). But it is only by use of some argument such as that which I outline that

[7] Edwards, p. 70.

we can use (b) to support the analyticity claim. Now it may be that
Edwards has some stronger premiss than (b) in mind, and one such
stronger premiss I shall discuss below (see. p. 25). But the argument
as it stands is sufficiently confusing to deserve some attention.

The trouble with the argument from (a) and (b) to (e) arises
with ambiguity of the intermediate steps. There is certainly a sense
of (c) such that (c) follows from (b). And there is probably a sense
of (d) such that (e) follows from (d). But in these senses (d) does not
follow from (a) and (c), nor can there be any senses of these steps
which combine to preserve the entailments.

The easiest way of seeing this is to consider how the argument
would stand if instead of (c) we substituted the proposition:

(c′) The use of the word "reason" is such that it is doubtfully,
and perhaps contingently, true that I-evidence provides a
reason for an I-proposition.

Now, in the sense of (c) in which it is consistent with (c′) and
indeed follows from it, it seems to me that (c) does follow from (b),
and (d) interpreted correspondingly will follow from (c) and (a).
But then of course there will be no temptation to suppose that the
conclusion follows. The sense of (d) which is needed for it to entail
(e) is something much stronger:

(d″) The meaning of the word "reason" is such that I-evidence
provides a reason for an I-proposition simply in virtue of
"reason" having that meaning.

This proposition may be strong enough to entail the analyticity claim,
but not only does it not follow from (c′), it is clearly inconsistent
with it. I say that it may be strong enough to entail the analyticity
claim since it is hardly clear enough what it means for its
entailment relations to be transparent, and no satisfactory account
of the relation between 'analytically true' and 'true in virtue of the
meaning of constituent terms' exists. Fortunately we need not investigate the relation between (d″) and (e). It is sufficient to notice
that (d″) cannot follow from (c) in that sense in which (c) follows
from (b), for since (c′) is consistent with (a) and (b), and inconsistent
with (e), (e) cannot follow from (a) and (b) alone.

The reason for the breakdown of the argument is easily seen.
(c′) is quite consistent with (a) and (b) because the "meaning = use"
thesis is quite consistent with some selectivity about those features

of use which are to be taken as determining meaning: in any sense in which it is true it does not entail that every feature of a use is *necessarily* a feature of that use, so that to question or deny *anything* which we normally say is to use some word in a different way, with a different meaning.

So far as I can see this is Edwards's only argument for the analyticity claim. But Strawson presents a *prima facie* different and better case for the same claim. He says:

> "And suppose someone were asked what he meant by saying that he had good grounds or reasons for holding [a belief expressible in the form 'Every case of *f* is a case of *g*']. I think it would be felt to be a satisfactory answer if he replied: 'Well, in all my wide and varied experience I've come across innumerable cases of *f* and never a case of *f* which wasn't a case of *g*.' In saying this, he is clearly claiming to have *inductive* support, *inductive* evidence, of a certain kind, for his belief; and he is also giving a perfectly proper answer to the question, what he meant by saying that he had ample justification, good grounds, good reasons for his belief."[8]

Now there is a sense of the word "means" in which if this answer Strawson gives *is* a satisfactory answer to the question "What do you mean by saying you have good grounds or reasons for believing this generalisation?" then it is analytic that inductive evidence is a reason for such a belief. This sense is that in which asking someone what he means is asking him what he is asserting, or asking him for an analysis or explication of what he is asserting. But it is not clear that if the question is intended in that sense, the answer Strawson cites is a satisfactory answer. For it would be a satisfactory answer to the question in that sense if and only if it is analytic that inductive evidence is a reason for a generalisation, and just asserting that it is a satisfactory answer is not providing an argument for that claim. But, it will be replied, surely it *is* plausible to suppose that the answer he gives is a satisfactory answer to the question? I think it is, but only because the question "What do you mean by saying that you have good grounds. . ." is seldom if ever used as a request for an analysis, but much more often as a request to produce those grounds. "What do you mean by saying that you have evidence that he is a thief?" As such a question is normally put I think it would be felt to be a perfectly satisfactory answer if I replied that I saw him running around in the night with a jemmy. But in giving such an answer I am clearly not expressing what is *meant* by saying that I have evidence that he is a thief, if for no other reason than that I can easily imagine having such evidence without having seen him running around in the night with a jemmy. The situation is again similar in moral discussion. "What do you mean by saying that he is a good man?" is usually answered simply by giving some of the evidence that he is a good man.[9] But this is not a good argument for naturalism, because here also the question is used as a request for evidence, not as a request for an explanation of the concept of evidence, or goodness.

There is a possible retort here, however. It could be argued that my alleged distinction between asking for an analysis and asking for grounds for the belief will not bear any weight. In the case of having evidence that someone is a thief, there is a clear distinction between citing the evidence (that one saw him in the night with a jemmy) and saying what is meant by the assertion that one has such evidence. As I pointed out, it is impossible to regard 'I saw him in the night with a jemmy' as meaning the same as 'I have evidence that he is a thief', since it is clearly logically possible that either should be true and the other false. But argument might be adduced that in the case of induction, or that of ethics, there is no distinction between asking for the grounds habitually given for a judgement, and asking for an analysis of the concept of a reason for that judgement. We shall consider this position later as an objection to supposing that my own account of the concept of being a reason for an I-proposition reinstates the problem of induction.[10] For the present all that we need note is that the question "What do you mean by saying that you have good grounds for *p*?" can certainly bear two different senses, as the case of the thief shows, and that we are given no reason in the passage from Strawson for supposing that the "satisfactory answer" answers the question in the relevant sense. In other words, either Strawson's question is a demand for an analysis, in

---

[9] Cf. Urmson's example in *The Emotive Theory of Ethics*, 1968, p. 79: "By a square meal I mean roast beef and Yorkshire pudding." As Urmson rightly says, nobody is going to take the word "square" to have as a rare meaning 'consisting of roast beef and Yorkshire pudding'.

[10] See below, pp. 24ff.

which case nothing has been done to show that the answer is satisfactory, or it is a demand for the man to cite his reasons, in which case the satisfactoriness of his answer does not entail that it is analytic that his knowledge is a reason. Either he has simply assumed the analyticity claim to be true, or he is using the fact that we give inductive reasons as an argument for its being analytic that such knowledge is a reason.

Given that the arguments advanced for it are not compelling, is the analyticity claim at all plausible, and ought we to admit its truth and "dissolve" the problem of induction as I am considering it? That Edwards himself has an awareness that the matter is not so easy is indicated in the following passage. After citing an inductive principle, roughly in the form that the more the inductive evidence the less often does it turn out that the next instance is false, he continues:

> ". . . it [this principle] does seem to me part of the *reason* for every inductive conclusion. I mean by this that we would not apply 'reason' to a large number of positive and widely varied instances if the contrary of the inductive principle were true or nearer the truth than the inductive principle."[11]

Now, what are we to make of this if it is analytic that a large number of positive and widely varied instances are a reason for an I-proposition, analytic because this is what "reason" means in this context? It is of course consistent with the analyticity claim to admit that it is contingent that the word "reason" means what it does, contingent for example upon facts about the English language. It is analytic that a father is a male parent, but it is contingent upon the truth of many things that the word "father" means what it does, truths about the existence of the word and its use in English. But it is not this sort of linguistic fact that Edwards states the meaning of the word "reason" to depend upon. It is his empirical principle about the greater probability of an inductively supported prediction being true. But it is extremely mysterious that an apparently linguistic fact should depend upon a principle of this sort. Certainly, if the phrase "reason for an I-proposition" has a separate sense, it may depend upon empirical probability principles that a large number of positive and widely varied instances fall

[11] Edwards, p. 73.

under the notion it expresses. But if this phrase is just *given* its sense as referring to a large number of positive and widely varied instances, then how should the rationality of its being given *that* sense depend upon empirical probability principles? So long as we take care to avoid duplications, unclarities, puns, and to remember, and to publicise, what we have done, we can with equal rationality give any hitherto unused sign what sense we like. It is only if the phrase "reason for an I-proposition" has a separate sense that it becomes rational or irrational, correct or incorrect, to describe a large number of positive instances by it. Similarly it is only if the word "cantilever" has a separate sense (as it has) that there arises a real question of whether the Forth Bridge falls under the concept it expresses, and so a question of the rationality of describing the bridge by means of it. Otherwise we could define the sign to refer to the bridge, or not, as we please. In short, what Edwards wanted to say here was that if the empirical principle were false, I-evidence would not be a reason for an I-conclusion. But he could not say this, because he believes that the analyticity claim is true; he could not say this any more than one could say that if certain empirical things were different, fathers would not be male parents. And so he has to make the incredible claim that there is an empirical, non-linguistic question whether a phrase which means something, should mean it. This is just like saying that there is a real question whether it is rational to call my dog "Rex" although the word has here no descriptive force at all.

The reinstatement of the problem

This mistake is important partly because Edwards makes it while trying to explain something which would be extremely strange if the analyticity claim were correct, namely that whenever any class of evidence is offered as a reason for a belief, people think that there is a proper question as to what it is in virtue of which it is a reason. I am not just repeating that some people have thought there was a problem where Edwards and Strawson think there is none, but drawing attention to the difficulty of *accounting* for their thinking this if the analyticity claim is correct. Philosophers certainly haven't thought that they were discussing whether inductive evidence is inductive evidence, and what they thought they were discussing instead is best seen by considering what questions would remain if the Strawson–Edwards account of the concept of reason were correct. It would of course no longer be necessary to ask for a justification for supposing that I-evidence is a reason for an I-proposition, but there are other questions: are beliefs for which we have a reason more probable than those for which we have none? Are the reasons ever strong enough to make it certain or even probable that they are true? And above all, why ought we to place any more confidence in I-propositions for which we have a reason, than in those for which we have none? Remember that upon their account "reason" as it occurs in these questions is synonymous with "knowledge of instances of the same phenomenon", and it immediately appears not only that these questions remain for Edwards and Strawson, but that they are very similar, if not identical, to the problems other philosophers have discussed by asking whether or not inductive knowledge provides a *reason* for beliefs. In particular I now want to concentrate upon the last question which remains for Edwards and Strawson, the question "Why ought we to place any more confidence in I-propositions for which we have a reason, than in those for which we have none?"

It is the third objection to the view that the Strawson–Edwards account of the concept of reason gives a dissolution of the problem of induction, that this question remains even if their analysis of the concept of reason is correct. For, suppose that someone convinces a sceptic about induction that as the word "reason" is normally used there can be no question about whether knowledge of varied positive instances is a reason for an I-proposition, that it is analytic that this is so. He can quite properly reply, if convinced of this: "Yes, I was wrong in presenting my sceptical doubts and arguments as raising doubt about the supposition that I-evidence is a reason for an I-proposition, for I now see clearly that this is analytically true. This being so, a correct description of what my sceptical arguments show would be that perhaps we ought to have no more confidence in an I-proposition for which we have a reason, than in one for which we have none." This reply is available to him if the Strawson–Edwards account is correct, and this by itself shows that their account does not solve or dissolve the problem of the justification of increasing confidence in a proposition given other knowledge of a certain sort.

But there is another point here. We have seen that *if* their analyticity claim is correct the demand for justification would be properly expressed by asking why we ought to have more confidence in a proposition for which we have a reason of a certain sort, than in one for which we have none. But that the question would be properly expressed in this way is itself an objection to the analyticity claim. For it seems extremely odd to ask why we ought to have more confidence in beliefs for which we have a reason than in those for which we have none. But it is not at all odd to ask why we ought to have more confidence in beliefs for which we have certain sorts of evidence, than in those for which we do not have evidence of this sort. I shall try to put this point in a clearer way.

Suppose a reductive account of the concept of reason were correct – that is, an account according to which to say that I have a reason for a belief is *just* to say that I have knowledge of some sort. Then there would arise *two* problems of justifying an increase in confidence in a belief: firstly show that you have a reason, secondly show that you ought to increase your confidence in the belief upon coming to possess a reason. But it is extremely hard to believe in this duality of problems. For if one thing is clear in the normal use of the word "reason", it is that once you have really shown that you have a reason for a belief, you need do nothing more to justify taking the reason as relevant to the amount of confidence to have in that belief. We often discuss whether evidence of some sort really is a reason for a belief, but once that question is settled, there is no further question whether this reason is *relevant* to the amount of confidence which we can justifiably place in the belief. The Strawson–Edwards account of the concept of reason is wrong in that it closes the first question – making it analytic that certain sorts of evidence are reasons for a certain sort of belief, and opens the second question – making it necessary to show why we should take these reasons as relevant to the amount of trust which we ought to place in our beliefs.

All this suggests very strongly that some normative account of the concept of reason is correct. For unless there is an equivalence in meaning between a proposition being a reason for another and it being correct to take the first as relevant to the amount of confidence which we ought to have in the second, there will be these two different problems of induction: show that I-evidence is a reason for an I-proposition, *or* show why I should take I-evidence into account in determining whether to place much confidence in an I-conclusion. In the next chapter therefore I shall propose and discuss in some detail a normative analysis of the concept of reason for a belief, and also discuss the way in which this reinstates the problem of justifying induction. For certain philosophers might hold that even if the Strawson–Edwards analysis of the concept of a reason does not by itself dissolve the problem, still, their method can be applied to a normative analysis to show that even if that is true, there is still no problem.

2

The analysis of reasons

A normative account

The idea of a normative account of the concept of a reason for a proposition is not new; it was proposed for example by Chisholm,[1] and is implicit in Urmson.[2] But their expositions leave scope for detail and it is the purpose of this chapter and the next to provide this. I shall take the following analysis as the basis of discussion:

(A) To say that P is a reason for Q is to say that it is right to have more confidence in Q upon coming to know P than before coming to know P, or would be right to do this if not already certain that Q is true or that Q is false, or as certain as evidence like P can make one.

The counterfactual clause in (A) covers the case of reasons for propositions in which there is no question of altering our confidence. For example, that there is a carpet in my rooms now is something of which everybody who comes in is justifiably certain, and there is no question that they will increase their confidence in this upon learning that there has been one here every day this term. Nevertheless the proposition that there has been one here every day this term is a reason for believing that there is one here now. It is not one of *my* reasons for believing that there is one here now, because I suppose myself to have conclusive sensory evidence for this; but it is incorrect to conclude that therefore it is not a reason for this at all. Again we can imagine cases in which one thing is a reason for another, although, while uncertain of the conclusion, we yet have enough evidence of that sort for this further acquisition to be of no use to us. So the counterfactual clause of the analysis is necessary. Fortunately in the case of inductive reasoning we can nearly always ignore it: it is necessary for accuracy but not important to the substance of the problem.

[1] Chisholm, *Perceiving*, 1957, p. 5.
[2] Urmson, "Some Questions Concerning Validity", in *Essays in Conceptual Analysis*, ed. Flew, 1963.

Some philosophers might be inclined to dismiss (A) not so much on the grounds that it is false, as on the grounds that it is misleading, misleading because it implies a false assumption about the way in which the sentence "it is right to have more confidence . . ." works. For it implies that this sort of sentence expresses a proposition, i.e. something true or false, whereas many people believe that such sentences are not used to express propositions, but to do other things. Now perhaps such an objection deserves a fuller reply,[3] but at present I shall just say this: that what I shall say for or against this propositional identity is easily construed as drawing attention to the similarities between saying that it is right to increase one's confidence under certain circumstances, and saying that it is reasonable to do so, independently of whether saying either of these things is construed as expressing something which is true or false. In other words, the adoption of a non-propositional account of normative language does not vitiate the discussion.

There is however another blanket objection to my sort of proposal which cannot be evaded so easily, and discussion of which takes us to the heart of the approach which "dissolves" the problem. This objection is that my analysis (A) really fails to provide an alternative to the Strawson–Edwards account of the notion of 'reason'. Instead it might be held that it is consistent with such an account. For it could be held that the word "right" has a meaning which varies from context to context, and that while it may be true that to say that an assertion is a reason for an I-proposition *is* to say that it is right to increase confidence, etc., this is simply because to say that it is right to increase confidence, etc., is itself to say only that there is I-evidence for the proposition. So that to say that we have a reason for an I-proposition again reduces, but via the normative analysis (A), to saying that we have I-evidence for it. This answer would be given by the revised form of naturalism which Edwards himself proposes,[4] whereby the proposition expressed by using evaluative words is just that expressed by stating the natural facts in virtue of which we believe whatever we are evaluating to be good or bad, right or wrong. A consequence of adopting this position would be that my third objection to the Strawson–Edwards account, which I presented at the end of the last chapter, would no longer

[3] I attempt to defend a propositional account of evaluative discourse in "Moral Realism", in *Morality and Moral Reasoning*, ed. Casey, 1971.

[4] Edwards, *The Logic of Moral Discourse*, 1955, ch. VII.

exist. For I there claimed that this account leaves open the question: "Why ought we to have more confidence in beliefs for which we have a reason, than in those for which we have none?", and with the reductive account of 'right' and 'ought' this question will again collapse.

This is nearly the view taken by Urmson. In his article he discusses the "validity" of inductive arguments, rather than the notion of inductive reasons, but the situation is the same. He finds that validity is an evaluative notion and says:

> ". . .we may expect there to be factual criteria or standards for its use, whether implicit or explicit, and these criteria will have a close logical connexion not amounting to identity of meaning with the evaluative term itself. . .If we want to know what these standards are, we can only find out what these standards or criteria are if we examine what are agreed to be valid and invalid arguments and elicit the criteria from them. . .if we can elicit from the usage of a group a set of criteria for the validity of a certain kind of argument, then it is pointless to ask whether *for that group* there is any distinction between valid and invalid arguments of the kind in question."[5]

Urmson takes the connection of meaning between the evaluative term and the criteria on which it is based to be so close that to doubt whether an argument is valid if it satisfies the criteria for *our* group is "ridiculous", or "bogus". So taking Urmson's view, and accepting the analysis (A), someone could hold that the meaning of "right to increase confidence in an I-proposition" is close enough to that of the standard or criterion for it, "possessing I-evidence", to make "bogus" any alleged doubt about whether someone who possesses I-evidence can rightly increase confidence in an I-proposition.

We can now see the stronger premiss which might be added to the argument on p. 14. The argument could become:

(a) Meaning = use.
(b) I-evidence is used as a standard or paradigm of the sort of evidence which gives a reason for, i.e. makes it right to increase our confidence in, an I-proposition.

[5] "Some Questions Concerning Validity", pp. 128–9.

(c) The use of "reason" (analysed perhaps as in (A)) is such that I-evidence provides a standard example of something which gives a reason for an I-proposition.

(d) The meaning of "reason" is such that I-evidence provides a standard example of something which provides a reason for an I-proposition.

(e) It cannot be doubted without convicting oneself of not knowing the meaning of "reason" or some other term that I-evidence provides a reason for an I-proposition.

By strengthening the premiss (b) and weakening the conclusion slightly we have transformed the argument into something much more like the standard "paradigm case" argument. Quite clearly the degree of weight that can be attached to it depends upon the relation between the meaning of evaluative terms, and standards or paradigms of things to which they apply. For (e) to follow from (d) this relation must be so close that the question of whether we are justified in using the standard examples which we do use cannot sensibly be raised. Now this is, of course, directly the point at issue, for if such a doubt can sensibly be raised, then there is a problem of justifying induction, and if it can't then there isn't such a problem. There are two objections, which are together quite conclusive, against supposing that the relation is so close. The first is that used by Moore against naturalism in ethics.

Moore's argument

Naturalism claims that there is an analysis of moral concepts: this means that there is some natural feature F such that to say that something is good is to say that it is F. If this is so, then it seems to follow that to doubt whether something is good is to doubt whether it is F. And if this is so then to doubt whether something which is F is good is to doubt whether something which is F is F.[6] But, says Moore, there is no natural property which can be shown to make these two doubts the same. The one is always a substantive moral perplexity, the other trivial, or, in a slightly extended sense, senseless.

[6] A precise analysis of what this means is given in Lewy, "G. E. Moore on the Naturalistic Fallacy", reprinted in *Studies in the Philosophy of Thought and Action*, ed. Strawson, 1968.

In the present case the argument would look like this. Take firstly the position which analyses 'this is something which makes it right to increase confidence in the I-proposition Q' as saying 'this is I-evidence related to the I-proposition Q'. Then to doubt whether this is something which makes it right to increase confidence in the I-proposition Q is to doubt whether this is I-evidence related to the I-proposition Q. And to doubt whether this, which is I-evidence related to Q, makes it right to increase confidence in Q is to doubt whether this, which is I-evidence related to Q, is I-evidence related to Q. But, echoing Moore, we can see that these two doubts are not the same. For it is plain that the first is a sensible doubt, in a way in which the second is not, but is trivial, or senseless.

The argument is simpler against those who give, not an analysis, but a version of Urmson's position, and accept an entailment from (d) to (e). For they think that doubt whether P, which is I-evidence related to Q, makes it right to increase confidence in Q, is a bogus doubt, and the reply is that on the contrary it is a sensible doubt.

Now this, of course, has a flavour of begging the question, and most philosophers confronted with Moore's argument in its ethical application, or again here, think that it begs the question, or at least worry whether it begs the question. It seems to me quite plain that it does not. The idea that it does arises from noticing that the person proposing the analysis *can* deny, and of course is committed to denying, that the two doubts which Moore has distinguished really are different. He *can* say that if someone doubts whether something which is *F* is good, where *F* is the favoured natural property, he is senselessly doubting whether something which is *F* is *F*, whatever he takes himself to be doing. And he *can* say that if someone doubts whether P, which is I-evidence related to Q, makes it right to increase confidence in Q, he is doubting whether P which is I-evidence related to Q, is I-evidence related to Q. But from the fact that he *can* say these things, it does not follow that Moore's argument in any sense begs the question. For identifying these doubts is to most people less plausible than giving the analysis. And to point out an implausible consequence of a position, even if it can be accepted by the strong-minded, is to give a good argument, not a question-begging argument, against that position. And what is more, Moore has things the right way round, and the philosopher maintaining the analysis has not. For it is sounder to use knowledge of which propositions can be doubted as an indication of which analyses are true, than it is to use assertions that some analyses are true to dictate which propositions can be doubted. What we doubt, just as much as what we say, is part of the evidence on which analyses must be based. This is especially so if, as in the induction case, all the other arguments for the analysis are very bad. To argue otherwise is precisely parallel to, say, adopting the view that to be reasonable is the same thing as to be voluble, and claiming that contrary evidence is illusory, and that in any case its use begs the question.

Still, I think it must be admitted that use of Moore's argument by itself leaves the matter in an unsatisfactory state. For even if, on reflection, we can see that there is a real doubt whether I-evidence is something which makes it right to increase confidence in a related I-proposition, and that the existence of this doubt is a good enough datum to destroy certain theories of the meaning of the proposition doubted, still we have no real understanding of what is being questioned, or how the doubt could arise or be settled. This leads into my second argument, one which needs to be added to Moore's argument to make the position conclusive. It explains why, in the case of induction, Moore's argument is a good one. I can introduce this by considering one author who has found the lack of explanation of how real doubt is possible a reason for denying that Moore's argument has any force at all.

L. J. Cohen says that one of the principal arguments for the Strawson–Edwards approach is that it is "senseless to ask whether the use of inductive standards is justified unless we can say to what other standards we are appealing for this justification. . .".[7] Then the trouble with attempting to reinstate the problem by stressing the normative nature of the concept of a reason, or validity, is that:

> "It gives no answer at all to the argument from the need for standards, since it does not say how we can tell whether something is a good or bad reason for accepting the principles by which we count as valid those inductive arguments that we do count as valid. Perhaps you can judge my ethical standards by appealing to your own. But how do you judge the inductive standards that seem common to all reasonable men? This question is crucial for any attempt to invoke here an analogue of Moore's argument against proposals to define 'good' in terms of some describable characteristic."[8]

[7] Cohen, *The Implications of Induction*, 1970, p. 185.   [8] Ibid. p. 186.

Now it is a profound misunderstanding of Moore's argument to suppose that it depends upon the existence of conflicting ethical standards. What it depends upon is the possibility of sensibly asking whether one's standards are correct, and this possibility can be seen to exist whether or not all men share the same standards, and whether or not one has in mind a conflicting set of standards by which to judge one's own. The possibility of sensibly asking whether one's standards of evidence are good ones does *not* arise only with possession of other, possibly better, standards against which to judge them: it arises if one apprehends the *logical possibility either* that there should be better standards, *or* that the situation is such that no standards are applicable. Let us now see where this logical possibility arises.

Firstly, we shall imagine a game played with a set of I-propositions. This game is called the Assessing Game, and is played as follows. In the game beliefs are judged as "Assessed-good", "Assessed-bad", "Assessed-better" (than another), and so on. A round of the game starts with the two players picking a separate I-proposition, and the object of the game is to establish that one's own proposition is Assessed-better than one's opponent's. To this end the players take turns, and each turn consists in either producing a piece of I-evidence appropriate to one's own I-proposition, or in destroying a piece of I-evidence produced on any previous turn by one's opponent, either by showing it to be false, or showing it to be inappropriate to his proposition. A round stops when both of the players have to pass, and the total they have accumulated according to some system of scoring determines which proposition is Assessed-better.

With a little more detail this might be quite a good game, although rather a highbrow one. Let us suppose that we did work out a viable system of scoring, awarding increased points say for quantity and variety of instances mentioned in the I-evidence, allowing indirect I-evidence, and so on. Now consider the meaning of the term "Assessed-better". This is surely given its meaning by the rules of the game: its meaning, so far as I can see, will correspond exactly with what Strawson and Edwards take "better grounded" to express. It would be completely silly for a philosopher to be given the rules of the game, and then to express a doubt at the end as to whether the I-proposition which satisfies the rules for being Assessed-better is *really* Assessed-better: satisfying those rules is just

what "Assessed-better" means, and that's the end of it. That is how
the Assessing Game is played.

The Strawson–Edwards theory gives an account of inductive
reasoning which makes it something equivalent to playing the
Assessing Game, albeit informally, and sometimes by oneself. The
Urmson position in the form which accepts the argument of p. 25,
makes it something like this, with the added interest that we somehow approve of those I-propositions which come out well in the
game. In either case, doubt about whether those propositions are
well grounded is precisely as silly as the corresponding question
for the Assessing Game.

It should I think be clear that this is a hopelessly bloodless view
of reasoning. For we have given no reason at all for anybody to
be *interested in* the Assessing Game, for anybody to apply the results of the game, or have more confidence in those propositions
which are Assessed-better than in those which are Assessed-worse.
Some players may acquire an attitude of approval to propositions
which win. But this might be just that they delight in them, or
relish them in the way one might relish a winning hand at cards.
And if they evaluate them as being worthy of confidence, or true,
or probably true, then this is something which is independent
of the game, and something which the mere existence of the game
does not by itself justify. In short, something is ignored in a
view which assimilates 'a proposition for which there is more
reason' to 'an Assessed-better proposition': the fact that reasoning
is analytically the instrument for matching our confidence with
truth.

We may now return briefly to the question of standards raised by
L. J. Cohen. We saw that the sense of the demand for a justification
of induction depended upon the apprehension of an apparent logical
possibility: the possibility either that there should be better standards,
or that no standards should be applicable at all. We can now see
where this possibility arises. It arises because we judge from the
standpoint of the success of reasoning in discriminating truth from
falsehood. There is a purpose in reasoning – to give us the truth,
and the demand we make of a use of reasons is that it should be
appropriate to this purpose. It is not that we have better *standards*
of reasoning, but that there is an external *standpoint* from which to
judge an allegedly good process of reasoning. This makes clear the
difference of that much-canvassed analogy, the question 'Is the law

legal?', for perhaps there is no standpoint outside the law from which the legality of the law can be judged.

The standpoint of achieving the truth

We must now try to see how the fact that there is a purpose in reasoning, and therefore a standpoint from which to judge its success, affects our understanding of the problem whose existence it assures. To do this we shall start by considering its effect upon the analysis (A) of the concept of one proposition being a reason for another (p. 23). The first reaction to the introduction of the notion of truth might be to try to construe the analysans in (A) as a disguised conditional. 'P is a reason for Q' would then be: '*If* one is to have confidence in true propositions *then* it is right to increase confidence in Q upon coming to know P, etc.' But this either will not do, or must be understood in such a special way that a reformulation is desirable. For we need but reflect that sometimes if we are to have confidence in true propositions we should not let the knowledge that P alter our confidence in Q, even although it is a reason for Q – namely in those circumstances in which $\sim Q$ is in fact true. For example, suppose that it is uncertain whether it is raining in the Lake District. We come to know that there is a depression centred on the Isle of Man, and this is a reason for supposing that it is raining in the Lake District. Now let us suppose that surprisingly, and unknown to us, it is not raining in the Lake District. Then it might be said that although knowledge of the depression is a reason for supposing it to be raining there, nevertheless if we are to have confidence in true propositions, it is *not* right to increase our confidence that it is raining upon coming to know of the depression, precisely because it is false that it is raining. So this hypothetical will not do as any analysis of one proposition being a reason for another. Its trouble is that it ties us too closely to success on the particular occasion of reasoning, yet everyone knows that our reasoning may be very good, yet our confidence judiciously placed in what is, unluckily, false.

This encourages us to adjust the hypothetical to render the actual truth or falsehood of the conclusion – which is precisely what we do not know and what we are reasoning about – irrelevant. All we demand is that a process of reasoning should be reliable, should be generally liable to lead to true belief. So we could try the following expansion of the normative account: '*If our confidence is to be adjusted in a way which generally furthers accord with the truth,* then it is right to have more confidence in Q upon coming to know P than before coming to know P, or would be. . .etc.'

This seems to be to be quite a good way of incorporating into our analysis the necessary truth that reasoning is conducted to find the truth, and certainly the generality we have introduced is needed for any such attempt. But it is not without perplexities of its own. In the first place, does it really give an explanatory identity, an analysis, of the normative element in (A)? It certainly appears to do so initially. For the bare assertion that it is right to increase confidence in one proposition upon coming to know another is certainly puzzling: is it a moral claim? Or what other sort of evaluation is being advanced? And we appear to remove this puzzle by explaining that all that is meant is that this sort of adjustment of confidence generally furthers accord with the truth. The puzzle might appear to be more definitively removed if we excised the word "right" altogether, and expressed the final account thus: 'If our confidence is to be adjusted in a way which generally furthers accord with the truth, then *we must* have more confidence in Q upon coming to know P, or it would be that we must if we were not. . .etc.' This appears to analyse what is meant by the introduction of the word "right". In a similar way someone might puzzle about the nature of the claim 'This is the right way to the Bodleian' and find relief in the plausible analysis 'If you are to get to the Bodleian (easily) then you must go this way.'

But the matter is certainly not as simple as this example indicates. Consider instead a genuinely moral use of "right", say in the proposition 'It is right to avoid creating unnecessary misery.' With the Bodleian example in mind, someone might offer as an equivalent 'If you are to be moral, then you must avoid creating unnecessary misery.' Now this is a poor analysis. For the first proposition might be expressed more forcibly as 'whether or not you are to be moral, it is right to avoid creating unnecessary misery': the point is that it is not to be analysed as a conditional, for just presenting the conditional misses out the point that some moral assessment attaches to whether you satisfy the antecedent. You can get rid of the necessity to go this way by deciding not to go to the Bodleian. But you cannot get rid of the necessity to avoid the creation of unnecessary pain by deciding not to be moral, for a moral verdict awaits any such decision.

Now in the same way it seems to me that a verdict of irrationality awaits the decision not to adjust our confidence in a way which generally furthers accord with the truth. It is completely up to us whether we want to go to the Bodleian or not, but it is not completely up to us whether we want to adjust our confidence in propositions in a way which generally furthers accord with the truth. If we don't do this we are irrational. So the attempt to cast light on the sense of "right" involved in the original analysis by the analogy of the analysis of 'This is the right way to the Bodleian' does not seem complete: standards of morality or rationality enable us to judge those who "choose" to be immoral or irrational, whereas knowledge of the route to the Bodleian does not enable us to guide or judge people who do not choose to go there. This shows that we don't fully understand the sense of "right" involved, because we have yet no account of the verdict 'it is right to adjust our confidence in propositions in a way which generally furthers accord with the truth'. This is true, and it is not the mere tautology that if our confidence is to be adjusted in a way which generally furthers accord with the truth then it must be adjusted in a way which generally furthers accord with the truth.

By what authority then might it be claimed that it is right to adjust our confidence in propositions in a way which generally furthers accord with the truth? We certainly don't want to lose sight of the suggested connection between the authority of reasoning and the authority of truth. To do so provides an open invitation to anyone who wishes to challenge the former, whether for a theological or for an even more woolly purpose. I suggest that we can keep this connection in sight like this. It is perfectly clear that a necessary connection between confidence and truth exists. It is to be hoped that what one has confidence in is true, and this is not contingent, as it might be, e.g., if one hoped that what one has confidence in is original or witty. One cannot intelligibly be described as reposing confidence in a proposition and being indifferent to its truth or falsehood. But if the connection between confidence and truth is accepted, we can accept the hypothetical analysis as a working tool, and still ask where the authority of reasoning, which on my account has just a *general* connection with obtaining the truth, arises. And the answer must come from a general defence of using on a *particular* occasion a strategy which *generally* furthers some aim. Only with such a defence could we answer somebody who says: "Of course I want to believe what's true. And you may show me that increasing confidence in an I-proposition upon coming to possess appropriate I-evidence is adjusting confidence in a way which generally furthers accord with the truth. Still, you can't show that it will on this occasion, so I might be right, I've no empirically false beliefs that you can show and I haven't contradicted myself, and in spite of the evidence I am going to go on reposing no confidence in the conclusion." The answer to this must wait until chapter 6, where the same problem arises for a different reason, and it is what is needed to complete the view that the authority of reasoning is nothing more, nor less, than the authority of truth. With this my remarks about the standpoint of achieving the truth and the final reinstatement of the problem of justifying induction end. Against Wittgenstein, we have denied that a good ground is one which looks like anything; it is one which does something, namely, gives us the right to expect success. A strong reason will have a connection with the truth which should greatly fortify our beliefs, a weak reason less, and a bad reason will perhaps be no reason at all, however often it is used as such.

Reasonable belief

We may now consider the consequences (A) has for the notion of a *reasonable belief*. If we hold (A) to be true it would be plausible to expect some parallel normative account of reasonable belief. A full discussion of the problem of induction needs to consider not only reasons for belief, but also reasonable belief itself, for, as I mentioned in the first chapter, we may be asked not only to justify taking I-evidence as a reason for an I-conclusion, but also to justify the large amount of confidence which we do place in some I-propositions as a result of such reasoning.

Now it certainly does not follow from the fact that I have a reason for a proposition that it is more reasonable for me to believe it than its negation: clearly my having a reason for something is consistent with my having more reason for its negation. But suppose that I have a reason for a proposition P, and do not have a reason or more reason for its negation $\sim$P. Does it then follow that it is reasonable for me to have more confidence in P than in $\sim$P? It may at first sight seem so, and some plausibility is lent to this by the consideration that instead of saying that it is reasonable to have more confidence in P than in ~ P, we may often simply say that there is more reason to believe P than ~ P. And if there is a reason for P and none for ~ P there certainly seems to be more reason for P than for ~ P.

But against this there is the following sort of case. It may apparently happen that a man has more reason for P than for ~ P simply because he *unreasonably* neglected to collect the evidence for ~ P. For example, suppose a man goes to watch a race between two horses. At the entrance a character of the turf tips one of them. I think we might agree that this is a reason, although a weak one, for expecting that horse to win, so that if the man knows nothing else about the two contestants, it is true that he has more reason for expecting that horse to win than to lose. So, according to the argument of the last paragraph, it might appear that it is reasonable of him to have more confidence that the tipped horse will win than not. But supposing he forms this confidence *unreasonably* neglecting to obtain further evidence. For example, suppose that it is perfectly obvious to everyone else at the race that one horse is extremely ill, or physically deficient, while the other is not, and suppose that the defective horse is the one that was tipped to the man, and suppose that he really ought to have noticed this, but failed to do so. I think we should say that here, although he had more reason for his belief than against it, it was nevertheless unreasonable of him to have more confidence in its truth than in its falsity, and this because it was unreasonable of him not to have come to realise the case against his belief. People often form unreasonable judgements not because they don't possess more reasons for them than against them, but because they unreasonably refused to show awareness, or become aware, of the evidence against their judgements.

I think therefore that a more accurate account of the relation between having a reason for a belief and having a reasonable degree of confidence in that belief, would be that it is reasonable to have more confidence in P than in ~ P if and only if there is more reason for P than against it and no evidence against P has been unreasonably ignored. The qualification that the evidence against P should have been *unreasonably* ignored is important. It is not enough for the confidence placed to be unreasonable that there should exist evidence against P which has *in fact* been ignored. Clearly a punter may, after due circumspection, rightly decide that he has more reason for supposing that a horse will win than he has for supposing that it will not, and reasonably place more confidence in this, even although there exists evidence that the horse will not win; even although, for example, the horse is secretly full of sedative. Here there exists evidence which the punter did not have, and could not reasonably have been expected to have, but it is quite consistent with this to suppose that his distribution of confidence was reasonable.

An interesting consequence of this account is that whether it is reasonable to have confidence in a proposition may sometimes depend in part upon what we are going to do with that confidence, or what we anticipate the consequences of our having such confidence to be. For if the consequences of our having misplaced confidence in a proposition are anticipated to be rather serious, then it may be unreasonable for us to fail to collect evidence, which, in a less serious situation, it might have been quite reasonable to fail to collect. In other words, whether a piece of evidence which could have been collected, but was not, was *unreasonably* ignored, may depend upon the gravity of the investigation. Suppose for example that A is casually assessing a pupil's ability. He remembers a good essay, a bright remark, not too many bad slips, and reasonably assents to the proposition that the student is quite able. But suppose B is to assess the same student's ability in order to judge him in a competition, say for a research grant, then it might be quite unreasonable for B to have confidence that he is quite able, remembering just the same facts. For B may reasonably be expected to go to more trouble to collect further evidence as to the student's ability. If this is extremely unfavourable and B failed to consider it, then B unreasonably had confidence that the student was able. This is a straightforward result of the fact that how much evidence we *should* collect is a function of the importance of coming to a correct conclusion.

Another consequence of this is the light it sheds on the so-called "paradox of ideal evidence".[9] The point may be put in the following way, taking an example of R. H. Vincent.[10] Suppose a man is told that he has a certain illness, and that three-quarters of the people with that illness die within a year. Suppose then that he learns further that he has an exceedingly specific form of that illness,

[9] Popper, *The Logic of Scientific Discovery*, 1968, p. 406 ('A Third Note').

[10] Vincent, "The Paradox of Ideal Evidence", *Philosophical Review*, 1962, p. 502.

and that three-quarters of the people with that form of the illness die within a year. The problem is that of describing what difference, if any, the acquisition of this further information should make to his confidence that he will die within the year. The paradox alleged by Popper is that according to many theories this evidence is irrelevant to the degree of confidence which the rational man would have in his dying within the year, yet, says Popper, surely this increase in the weight of the evidence must be relevant to *something*. The short answer is clearly that the confidence the man should have in the hypothesis remains the same, but that he should increase his confidence that this confidence is appropriate. In terms of probabilities, the probability of his dying remains the same relative to the new evidence, but the degree of confidence which may be attached to $\frac{3}{4}$ being *the* probability of his dying, goes up. With a different example, if we know nothing about a coin we may suppose that the probability of its landing heads is $\frac{1}{2}$ if we toss it from a fair device, and if we have tossed it a million times and it has landed heads exactly half of those times, we may also suppose the probability of its landing heads to be $\frac{1}{2}$, but with a great deal more confidence.

There is, however, a residual worry. For what is not clear is how a man's increasing his confidence that a high degree of confidence in an hypothesis is right, *falls short of* actually increasing confidence in the hypothesis. Mightn't the man actually increase his confidence in his imminent death upon coming to hear the news of the specific nature of his illness – isn't that news bad news for him? I think it is one of the virtues of our analysis that it shows quite nicely how this *may* be bad news for him.

Consider the case where the man is told that he has the illness, and that three-quarters of the people die within the year, but reasonably believes that there are different varieties of the illness with different death-rates. He certainly has a good reason for expecting to die within the year, but as I have argued, for him rationally to have a good deal of confidence in this, there must be no evidence which he has unreasonably failed to consider. Now it would be very reasonable of the man, who thinks that there is a chance of his having a less serious form of the disease, to want to gain the evidence about what form of disease he actually has before being prepared to repose a high degree of confidence in dying within the year. And if this evidence comes, and it turns out that he has not got a milder, nor a more serious, form, it may then and only then be reasonable for him to have confidence that he will die before the year is out, for only then has he considered the evidence which he should have considered.

On the other hand, if the man has no rational beliefs about the existence of different forms of the disease, or of known variations in people's susceptibility to it, or of anything which might become known and give him reason for hope, and it *then* comes to his notice that he has a form of the disease from which three-quarters of the sufferers die, it seems to me that his confidence should be entirely unaffected. Perhaps some of the difficulty of seeing this comes from the difficulty of imagining someone who wasn't aware of the fact that diseases have different forms, and strike different people more or less seriously.

It follows too that the strength of a reason, i.e. the amount by which it ought to increase one's confidence, may vary with its weight, i.e. the degree to which one thinks that it exhausts the evidence which ought to be taken into consideration. That is, we can preserve the intuitive idea that a weightier argument can be a stronger argument, an idea which has received scant respect since Keynes distinguished weight from degree of support.[11] Keynes was certainly right that there are cases – the coin-tossing example is one – where weight of evidence should not alter one's confidence in an hypothesis. But there are other cases. Consider two doctors, A and B, both with slightly more confidence in an hypothesis, say that someone who has our hypothetical disease will die within a year, than in its negation. Suppose further evidence comes that he has fainting fits, and that seven-eighths of those with fainting fits who have the disease die within a year. Let A consider this to be all the evidence that could be collected. But let B consider that other evidence about the man's state of health should be collected (believing perhaps that although fainting fits are statistically associated with the higher death-rate, this is just because they are often associated with something else which is causally important and should be investigated). Each doctor may be reasonable in his belief; B just knows more than A. It seems to be quite possible that on learning of the fainting fits it is reasonable for A to increase his confidence in the man dying *more* than it is reasonable for B to do: it is right for A, but not for B, to have great confidence, precisely because B rationally thinks that there is other evidence which should be col-

[11] Keynes, *A Treatise on Probability*, 1921, ch. VI.

lected. B can put a brave face on it to his patient without the resources of insincerity which A would need. So it seems to me a perfectly acceptable consequence of our analysis that a piece of information will be a stronger reason for one person than another in this situation. This is not of course to make the concept in any way subjective, for the strength of reason a new piece of knowledge provides depends upon what other beliefs the man *rationally* holds.

This discussion of the relation between having reasons for a belief and having a reasonable belief may seem unduly complicated. But this is an area in which it is difficult to go too slowly, and what I have said emphasises one important distinction, that between belief in a proposition being reasonable, and that proposition being probable. It is tempting to suppose that the reasonable degree of belief in a proposition is that which accords with its probability, so that if its probability is $\frac{1}{2}$ it follows that it is reasonable to have just as much confidence that it is true as that it is false. But in fact this is not so. For it may be perfectly reasonable for a punter to have great confidence that a horse will win, even although it is extremely probable that it will not. Sufficient conditions for it being reasonable for the punter to have more confidence that it will win than not, are that he should have more reason for this, and not have unreasonably failed to try to obtain evidence against it. But these are not sufficient conditions for it being probable that the horse will win. For, as we saw, there might exist excellent evidence that the horse will not win, even although the punter is not being unreasonable in failing to obtain it; and under these conditions it is not probable that the horse will win – it may be certain that he will not. Further consideration of the relation between the notions of 'reason' and 'probability' is given in chapter 5.

Of course, I am not denying that when it is reasonable to have more confidence in P than in $\sim$P it is also reasonable to believe that P is probable; indeed these two things may seem to be strictly equivalent.[12] But it may be reasonable to believe that P is probable without it being probable, and P may be probable without it being reasonable to believe that it is so. This is clearly of immense importance in the enterprise of justifying induction by means of showing that if certain things are true of the world certain hypotheses would have finite initial probabilities, and evidence would raise those

[12] But see below, chapter 5.

probabilities. For to show that induction is reasonable it would not only be necessary to discover that the conditions *might* obtain under which, say, some analogue of Bayes's theorem applies to give various conclusions large probabilities, it would be necessary to show that it is reasonable to suppose that they *do* obtain. Otherwise nature might be uniform, or independent variety limited, and certain hypotheses in fact probable, without it being at all reasonable to suppose that they are, or at all unreasonable to suppose that they are not.

I have given what appear to be the "detachment" conditions of the reasonableness of having more confidence in P than in $\sim$P, i.e. the conditions under which we not only know R and R is a reason for P, but also that it is reasonable to put trust in P: we may infer that it is reasonable to place more trust in P than in $\sim$P from the facts that there is more reason for P than $\sim$P and that we have not unreasonably failed to obtain any evidence for $\sim$P. It would tidy things up to be able to give an analysis of 'it is reasonable to have more confidence in P than in $\sim$P', corresponding to (A), and which entails the truth of this detachment condition. The immediate candidate for an analysis of 'it is reasonable to have more confidence in P than in $\sim$P' is simply the following:

(A*) To say that it is reasonable to have more confidence in P than in $\sim$P is to say that it is right to have more confidence in P than in $\sim$P.

And indeed I think that if (A*) is true, the detachment conditions which I have given are the correct ones. For remembering the analysis of 'P is a reason for Q' it appears that to say that there is more reason for a proposition than for its negation is to say that the evidence ought to increase confidence in P rather than in $\sim$P, and the conjunction of this with the proposition that no evidence for $\sim$P has been wrongly neglected does seem to entail that it is right to have more confidence in P than in $\sim$P.

The interest of this entailment is that by using it we seem to be able to ignore problems of *a priori* distributions of confidence. In order to obtain a justified level of confidence (greater in P than in $\sim$P) out of consideration of things which make it right to increase confidence, it has seemed to many that we need some claim about how, in advance of *all* reasons, our confidence in P and $\sim$P should be distributed. And by producing this entailment I seem to conjure away this notorious difficulty. But this seems to me to be a good thing. If we were not driven to it by misdirected theory, or worse still by metaphors of levels rising and falling, the concept of *the* reasonable amount of confidence to place in a proposition in advance of *any* reasons for it or against it would appear as silly as it is. Clearly where ignorance is total no policy for distributing confidence can be known to have any connection with the truth. Fortunately ignorance is never total, and there is no need to derive the rationality of a degree of confidence when we know relevant things, from the chimerical notion of what is reasonable when there exist absolutely no reasons.

There are one or two residual remarks to make about (A*) and the entailment which it justifies. As with (A) it is the nature of the normative concept which is puzzling. Of course we cannot construe the sense of "right" as one in which it is right to have more confidence in P than in $\sim$P if and only if P is true: this is the analogue of the point made on p. 31 above. But equally we have to preserve the connection between rightness and truth. The most attractive explanation is to suppose that the sense of "right" is derivative from the account of the notion of a reason which I gave. 'It is right to have more confidence in P than in $\sim$P' then says that a policy leading to such placing of confidence is a policy which generally yields the truth. That is, P is the outcome of a proper use of reasons[13] – for on p. 31 we established the view that using a reason must be an operation which generally gives the truth. With these explanations, the entailment claim that gives us our detachment conditions is this:

(X) The propositions which we know or reasonably believe (call their conjunction P) satisfy the condition that if our confidence is to be adjusted in a way which generally furthers accord with the truth, then it is right to have more confidence in Q upon coming to know P than before coming to know P

and

(Y) There are no other propositions which we should know or reasonably believe and which added to the conjunction P would falsify (X).

together entail

(Z) A policy which leads to the placing of confidence in Q rather than in $\sim$Q generally furthers accord with the truth.

[13] Or also of non-propositional "evidence of the senses".

And this seems as clear as any entailment between propositions involving such difficult notions could be.

If my account of the detachment conditions of 'it is reasonable to have more confidence in P than in ~ P' is substantially correct it clearly gives an answer to the relation between the two problems, that of justifying taking I-evidence as a reason for an I-proposition, and that of justifying placing more confidence in an I-proposition than in its negation. For if we can show that I-evidence is a reason for an I-proposition, at least in some cases, then it will be clear that it is reasonable to place more confidence in some I-propositions than in their negations. For in some cases it will be clear that we have no reasons for their negations, and also clear that this is not due to negligence. So in these cases we not only have a reason for the I-proposition, but are also justified in placing more confidence in it than in its negation.

The analysis also throws some light on the possible forms of scepticism which we might encounter. Let us suppose that we do use I-evidence to increase our confidence in I-predictions, and that as a result we are often confident in certain I-predictions. Common to all scepticism will be the belief that it cannot be shown or argued that this formation of confidence is the outcome of an operation which generally gives the truth. But different interpretations of this sceptical position are possible. Most philosophers would hold that it is wrong, in some sense, to be certain of a prediction, unless it is known that the policy of reasoning behind it *always* gives the truth. This is certainly not the case with inductive reasoning, and I shall not discuss whether we would be right to draw the consequence that certainty in its conclusions is therefore inappropriate. But what of high confidence? We can imagine at least three positions, in descending order of pessimism:

1. If, because of I-evidence, we have *any* particular degree of confidence in an I-proposition, from 0 to 1, we will be unable to show that we are confident to a degree appropriate to the general success of this sort of reasoning. For nothing at all can be shown about the general success of this sort of reasoning. So the only proper thing to do is to be indifferent to prediction: i.e. to withdraw our attention from the matter.

2. If, because of I-evidence, we have any particular *high* degree of confidence in an I-proposition, we will be unable to show

that we are confident to a degree appropriate to the general success of this sort of reasoning. For nothing at all can be shown about the general success of this sort of reasoning. So the only proper thing to do is to expect anything just as much as anything else; i.e. to have low confidence in any particular prediction.

3. If, because of I-evidence, we have any particular degree of confidence in an I-proposition, from 0 to 1, we will be unable to show that we are confident to a degree appropriate to the general success of this sort of reasoning. For nothing at all can be shown about the general success of this sort of reasoning. So *any* degree of confidence is equally permissible. There is no unique reasonable distribution of confidence, and no way of criticising any particular expectation anybody may hold.

There are difficulties with each of the first two positions. The first finds that we ought to disengage from thinking at all about the future. But it is not at all clear *why* we ought: my analysis leaves it impossible that this should be an "ought" of reason, because a policy of disengagement can have only a negative connection with placing confidence in what is true. Furthermore, it is not clear that we can be indifferent to a prediction in the sense of being neither certain nor very confident nor fairly confident that it is true nor certain nor very confident nor fairly confident that it is false. But if we must be one of these things, then the first position collapses into the second or the third.

The second position seems to be surreptitiously the most popular amongst philosophers. A philosopher is traditionally someone who uses his skill to make untutored confidence wilt, and the second view expresses this role nicely. If we think of the vast variety of things which could happen instead of an I-proposition being true, it is very tempting to suppose that the correct consequence of scepticism is that it is only reasonable to have low confidence in any particular prediction, and wrong to have high confidence in any. But why? To say this demands showing that *this* way of forming confidence has that general connection with success which is denied to inductive reasoning. But why suppose that it has? Unless the sceptic does the reverse of justification, and shows some connection between inductive reasoning and general *failure*, he is in no position to advocate some other distribution of confidence as uniquely reasonable.

So the third, liberal, sceptical position, is left as the best interpretation of a failure to justify inductive reasoning. This sceptic says that since no policy of forming confidence or varying it with the production of certain facts can be shown to have any general connection with the truth, we are entirely free to be as confident in any individual prediction, or in its negation, or as uncommitted, as we please. This seems to me to be the right position to attribute to a sceptic who claims the irrelevance of I-evidence to I-prediction, and since Hume held this, I shall call this opponent the Humean sceptic. He might of course augment his position by saying that on extra-rational grounds confidence in some predictions is to be preferred (say because surprises are less unpleasant than continued hesitation) or lack of confidence in any prediction is to be recommended (because some surprises are more unpleasant than judicious caution) but these things do not concern us.

In the next chapter I shall consider philosophically the formal properties of the relation given to us in the analysis of this chapter. For it is a striking property of the normative account and the connection with the purpose of gaining the truth which explains it, that it throws a certain amount of light on problems of support and confirmation. Whilst such formal work is of some intrinsic interest, and gives us certain principles to rely upon, and still more not to rely upon, it is like most formal work in making little direct contribution to the problem of justification. The next chapter could therefore be omitted by those who find logical issues uncongenial. Its principal philosophical point is to show how little connection exists between the notion of a reason and the notion of deducibility, or entailment. The result of this is that certain quite natural views about reasoning need to be abandoned, but this is a story which may be taken up again in chapter four.

3

The logic of increasing confidence

Introductory

The analysis (A) has stood up to some investigation as an account of the concept of one proposition being a reason for another. The purpose of this chapter is to go further into the logic of the relation which we have identified. We may symbolise this relation as follows:

$P R Q =$ df it is right to have more confidence in Q upon coming to know P than before coming to know P, or would be right to do this if not already rightly certain that Q is true or that Q is false.

Of course, this notion may be worthy of investigation independently of whether "P R Q" actually means the same as "P is a reason for Q". After all, what we are primarily interested in when we discuss questions of evidence is justified confidence, and even if the concept of reason turned out to be a complicated construction out of 'R', still investigation of situations where it is right to increase confidence could claim fundamental importance.

Similar remarks apply to the relation between 'P R Q' and 'P confirms Q'. We shall find many things which have been thought to be true of the confirmation relation, and which are certainly not true of 'R'. Where this is so we may take one of two courses. We may suppose that the author of the confirmation theory had a relation sufficiently like 'R' in mind for us to have shown his description of its behaviour wrong; or, more charitably, we may suppose him to have had a different relation in mind. But often when it is not the case that P R Q, it will be difficult to see in what sense if any P confirms Q.

I am treating 'R' as a relation between propositions, not sentences. This should scarcely need saying, but it is clear from the definition that 'R' holds between something we can have confidence in, and something we can come to know, and the general term for such things is "proposition". They are certainly not sentences, and indeed later in discussing Goodman's paradox we shall see that it is of the first importance to distinguish carefully the linguistic item from what it says. 'R' is not only a relation between propositions, but it is also quite certainly not a truth-functional one. That is whether or not P R Q holds cannot be determined simply by investigating the truth values of P and Q; some further connection must be exhibited.

P R Q thus expresses a non-truth-functional relation between P and Q. This is a relation, however, which holds contingently. For it is quite clear that in some circumstances it may be right to increase confidence in an hypothesis upon coming to know some proposition, whereas in other circumstances it might not have been right to do this. (From now on I shall restrict attention to propositions which are contingent and uncertain, in order to avoid repetition of the cumbersome counterfactual clause in (A), except where this restriction would affect the arguments.) The relevant feature of different circumstances will be the other propositions which I know or reasonably believe. Thus if I am possessed of some information it may be right for me to increase confidence in some hypothesis upon coming to know a particular proposition, whereas possessed of other information it would have been unjustifiable, and possessed of yet different information it might even have been right to increase confidence in the negation of the hypothesis. Consider for example:

(q) X has just obtained a cup of coffee.

X we suppose is sitting next to me in a restaurant, with a cup of brown liquid.

(p) X previously stated his intention of having a coffee.

(b_1) In most restaurants people usually get coffee when they ask for it, and there is no known reason for X to have changed his mind.

(b_2) In this restaurant tea and coffee are in fact distributed randomly in the same quantities, since in the way they are made here they are indistinguishable to taste.

(b_3) The waitresses in this restaurant habitually serve tea for coffee and vice versa, as a practical joke.

Usually if I know (b_1) then it is right to increase confidence in (q) upon coming to know (p). If I know (b_2) then coming to know (p) ought not to affect my confidence in (q). And finally, if I know (b_3) then it would be right to increase confidence in the negation of (q), and decrease confidence in (q), upon coming to know (p).

The basic relation with which we are concerned is therefore more accurately symbolised as "P R_s Q", defined as 'P R Q in situation s'. The relevant feature of the situation seems to be what else is known or rationally believed in it. So if we introduce the sign "R_s (P)" to mean 'It is right to have more confidence in (P) than in ($\sim$P) in situation s', we can define sameness of situation:

$$ s_1 = s_2 =_{df} R_{s_1}(P) \equiv R_{s_2}(P) $$

People may be inclined to suppose that the contingency of P R Q disqualifies it as an analysis of 'P is a reason for Q'. They might hold that in these cases it is wrong to say that whether 'P is a reason for Q' depends upon what else is rationally believed, but we should rather say that the conjunction of P and some background information is a reason for Q, and the conjunction of P and other background information not. If this has to be accepted, it is a disproof of our proposed analysis.

It seems to me, however, to be perfectly in order to say that in some circumstances P is a reason for Q, and in others not, and in yet others a reason for $\sim$Q. To hold otherwise is in effect to maintain that if there is a proposition C which conjoined with P gives a proposition which is not a reason for Q, then P is itself not a reason for Q, but only at best P and $\sim$C. To hold this to be true would be to deny that all the things we give as reasons actually are reasons. For example, if I give (p) as a reason for (q), this position would say that I am mistaken, that only (p) and the negation of (b_2) and (b_3) and a vast number of similar propositions provide a reason for (q). There doesn't seem much to be said for this. With entailment on the other hand it is certainly true that:

$$ (P \,\&\, C \looparrowright Q) \to (P \looparrowright Q) $$

and this is used in the best way of refuting an alleged entailment, namely that in which the addition of a premiss can be shown to destroy the appearance of an entailment.

We shall incline, then, to be suspicious of any claim that some sort of proposition is *necessarily* a reason for some other proposition, for the best that we could admit would be the necessity that 'in most cases', or 'other things being equal', or 'knowing what is usually known, but nothing more', P ought to increase one's confidence in Q. The view that P R Q is contingent when true stands opposed to the idea of a reason as something which 'partially entails' its conclusion, or as something which bears the relation it does to the conclusion simply in virtue of some connection of meanings. Thus in many confirmation theories the value of c(h, e), "the confirmation of hypothesis h upon evidence e", is supposed to depend entirely upon the predicates occurring in h, e.[1] As a defence against the possibility that mere addition of extra words to the language should alter the extent to which P is a reason for Q, this is admirable. But since the restriction forbids the acquisition of background information to raise or lower the value of c(h, e) unless the predicates involved are reinterpreted, the function cannot by an analysis of P R Q. Actually it is this very feature of Carnap's systems which opens them to Putnam's objection that we want to say that one law being confirmed may be a reason for another law when there exists a theory connecting them, although when there does not exist such a theory there is no connection of meanings which makes one a reason for another.[2] For us, P R Q expresses a relation between P and Q which holds according to whether a normative relation exists between coming to know that P and increasing confidence in Q; and the existence of this relation does not depend solely upon the meanings of P, Q, but, as we have seen, on the background information as well.

Reasons and entailment

Although P R Q may be true when there is no entailment between P and Q, it is not so obvious whether the existence of an entailment may not be sufficient for a reasoning relation to hold. So we may start by listing the two conjectural principles:

(CP1) $(P \rightarrow Q) \rightarrow (P R Q)$
(CP2) $(Q \rightarrow P) \rightarrow (P R Q)$

We need not use the notation "P R_s Q" in the statement of these, since if P entails Q it entails it in any situation. Since 'R' is a dyadic relation, and any member of its field may entail and be entailed by other propositions, we have in addition the following four conjectural principles:

[1] Carnap, *The Continuum of Inductive Methods*, 1952, § 11, p. 32.
[2] Putnam, " 'Degree of Confirmation' and Inductive Logic", in *The Philosophy of Rudolph Carnap*, ed. Schilpp, 1964, p. 781.

(CP3)   (P R_s Q) & (P→T) →(T R_s Q)
(CP4)   (P R_s Q) & (T→P) →(T R_s Q)
(CP5)   (P R_s Q) & (Q→T) →(P R_s T)
(CP6)   (P R_s Q) & (T→Q) →(P R_s T)

The first two state what is true if the reason has entailment relations, and the second two what is true if the consequent has entailment relations. Some of these principles have been much debated
in the literature. Hempel in his original articles christened (CP1)
"the entailment condition", (CP5) "the special consequence condition" and (CP6) "the converse consequence condition".[3] At that
time he viewed them as adequacy conditions upon any concept of
confirmation, i.e., no relation which failed to satisfy them could be
properly called a confirmation relation.

Before discussing these principles directly there is a point to
be made about entailment. It is quite possible for one proposition to
entail another without it being realised that it entails it. For example,
it is quite plausible to suppose that Peano's axioms for arithmetic
entail that every even number is the sum of two primes, or that they
entail that some even number is not the sum of two primes, but
nobody knows which. This is quite independent of the belief that
entailment is identical with the relation of strict implication, for even
if it is a stronger relation, it may plausibly be supposed to hold
between the axioms of arithmetic and other true arithmetical propositions. Furthermore it may be reasonable to suppose that an
entailment holds when it does not: it might be reasonable to suppose
that Peano's axioms entail that every number is the sum of two
primes (because, say, we have come very near to proving this
theorem, or even because Gödel or some other reliable source has
conjectured that it is true) when in fact they do not entail this but
the reverse. So we should ask whether in the statement of (CP1. . .6)
it is the condition that the entailments hold that we really want, or
the condition that it is reasonable to suppose that the entailments
hold. It seems to me that the case of Peano's axioms and Goldbach's
theorem shows that it is really the latter condition that is relevant.
For it may be right to increase confidence in Peano's axioms upon,
say, being taken through them by a logician and being shown how
they are modelled by zero and its suite, or perhaps upon being given
a consistency proof for first-order arithmetic. But then even if Peano's

---

[3] Hempel, "Studies in the Logic of Confirmation", *Mind*, 1945.

axioms do entail Goldbach's theorem or its negation, if we do not have any idea which, it would be quite wrong to increase confidence in either upon being reassured about Peano's axioms. It would seem then that we should discuss (CP1...6) only under the supposition that it is reasonably supposed that the entailments in question hold.

Although this may be satisfactory for our purposes, since in discussing reasoning in empirical matters we may assume that people recognise entailments correctly, the point has subtler implications. For suppose we were inclined to accept, say (CP5) in the form 'If P is a reason in s for Q, and it is reasonably supposed that Q entails T, then P is a reason in s for T.' And suppose further that we thought, as many logicians do, that entailment is identical with strict implication. Then of course if it was reasonable to suppose a certain proposition necessary, it would be reasonable to suppose that any other proposition entailed it. So if we have a proposition T, which it is reasonable to suppose necessary, then any proposition will be a reason for it. The same result comes from (CP1). But it is completely unacceptable to suppose that when I reasonably think, but am not certain, that a proposition is necessarily true, any other proposition whatsoever should increase my confidence in its truth. So if we are to preserve the idea of 'reasoning for or against a necessary proposition', which seems a rather strong desideratum, we shall have to deny that entailment is strict implication, or deny that 'R' is transitive over all entailment steps.

I shall henceforward suppose that when P→Q it is reasonably considered to do so, and vice versa, so that we need not continually interrupt the discussion to make this claim. As I say, it will not place any significant restriction on our account of reasoning in empirical matters. I shall now state three principles which are clearly true of 'R':

(L1) $P\,R\,P$
(L2) $(P\,R_s\,Q) \rightarrow\, \sim(P\,R_s\, \sim Q)$
(L3) $(EP)(EQ)(Es)(\sim(P\,R_s\,Q)\,\&\, \sim(P\,R_s\sim Q))$

The first of these is self-evident: it is universally right to increase confidence in P upon coming to know P. This might again be used as an objection to the analysis of reason in terms of 'R'. Surely propositions are not reasons for themselves? Well, it is certain that propositions are no use in reasoning for or against themselves; I cannot convince you of P by producing P, unless you are being irrational. But this seems to be a requirement on reasoning with someone, rather than upon the notion of a reason: it is open to us to say that P is a conclusive reason for P, although, because of its very strength, useless in reasoning to P. This seems preferable to attempting to place restrictions upon P and Q to limit cases where given P *R* Q, P is also a reason for Q, for such restrictions would have to cut a very fine path to leave some deductively valid reasons, but exclude P as a reason for P. (L2) says that if in a situation it is right to increase confidence in Q upon coming to know P, then it is not right to increase confidence in ~Q upon coming to know P. Increasing confidence in ~Q is the very same thing as decreasing confidence in Q, so (L2) says merely that for no P or Q can it be right to increase and decrease confidence in Q upon coming to know P. (L3) says that there are cases where one proposition is neither a reason for nor against another. We shall also assume a stronger version where Q ranges over propositions such that $R_s(Q)$: i.e., there are cases where coming to know one proposition ought not to increase or decrease confidence in a proposition which it is reasonable to believe.

(*CP1*) As I pointed out before, we cannot hold this and the view that entailment is strict implication. For take any proposition Q about which we are not certain, but which we reasonably and truly believe necessary. Then if the strict implication analysis is correct any proposition would be reasonably and truly believed to entail Q, so, by (CP1), upon coming to know any proposition whatsoever it would be right to increase confidence in Q, which is absurd. On the other hand, if we restrict attention to purely contingent propositions, (CP1) is unexceptionable. I should say in passing that the proposition 'If P and Q are uncertain and it is truly and reasonably believed that P entails Q then upon coming to know P you ought to increase confidence in Q' has enough plausibility in its own right to constitute an objection to the strict implication analysis. Fortunately, this pertains to the logic of entailment rather than that of reasoning.

(*CP3*) (I postpone discussion of (CP2), as it is best conducted when we have seen what other principles to accept). This principle is obviously false. For let I be any proposition irrelevant to Q – that there are such is assured by (L3). And let T be the disjunction,

(P v I). Then although P R_sQ, it need not be the case that (P v I) R_s Q, for we could come to know the disjunction by coming to know the irrelevant I. It would not then be right to increase confidence in Q. Lastly of course, P entails (P v I).

(*CP4*) This is also invalid. For if T is the conjunction of ~Q and P, the antecedent is satisfied, but by (CP1) and (L2), not the consequent. That is, (~Q & P) entails ~Q, so by (CP1), (~Q & P) R ~Q, and therefore by (L2), ~((~Q & P) R Q).

These two conditions have not to my knowledge been discussed in the literature. However it is interesting to note that (CP4) is a theorem for the notion of 'plausible implication' introduced by Rescher[4] and defined as:

> P plausibly implies Q if there exists a proposition which is likely to be true, which conjoined with P entails Q.

For by this definition, if P plausibly implies Q, then anything which entails P plausibly implies Q also. For if (P & R) entails Q, and X entails P, then (X & R) entails Q. There is a more obvious objection to the possible view that plausible implication provides an analysis of reason, namely that anything will plausibly imply a proposition which is itself likely. This Rescher notes as a "Paradox of Plausible Implication", from its obvious analogy to the paradox of material implication that a true proposition is materially implied by any proposition whatsoever. But as our strengthened (L3) reflects, it is quite absurd to suppose that it is right to increase confidence in a proposition which it is already reasonable to believe upon coming to know any other proposition at all: principles of relevance must be observed in arguing for any conclusions, even if they are already likely. Rescher does not present his notion as an account of 'being a reason for', and it cannot be taken as such.

(*CP5*) This is the "special consequence condition". It is important to try to establish the truth about this and (CP6) independently. For although it has long been known that acceptance of both of them conflicts with (L3), it is not so clear which one ought to be rejected. I shall argue they are both false, and that no straightforward restrictions can preserve them. I shall firstly present two sorts of case which provide counterexamples to (CP5).

[4] Rescher, "Plausible Implication", *Analysis*, 1961, p. 128.

Suppose that I am presented with an apparently symmetrical die, and told nothing about it. There are six possible hypotheses about which way it will fall, and no reason for having more confidence in one than in another. This is the antecedent situation. I then come to know that this die was made by Luigi, who always weights his dice to come down five or six uppermost. This evidence I call P. It is right for me to increase confidence in H_1 that the die will come down six uppermost, and H_2 that the die will come down five uppermost, upon coming to know P. These two possibilities are each favoured by the evidence as against the other four. But H_1 entails the negation of H_2. So $(P R_s H_1)$ & $(H_1 \rightarrow \sim H_2)$. But $\sim (P R_s \sim H_2)$, for, on the contrary, $(P R_s H_2)$, and (L2) forbids it to bear the relation to both an hypothesis and its negation. In other words, our knowledge of Luigi's chicanery makes it right to increase our confidence in each of these hypotheses, yet the fulfilment of one is logically inconsistent with the fulfilment of the other. So the antecedent of (CP5) is satisfied, but not the consequent.

Hacking in presenting Koopman's logic of comparative support as a basis for his work, discusses a similar case in which the central point is that two mutually inconsistent hypotheses are each supported by the evidence, as against other hypotheses.[5] Because Koopman's logic has a principle of implication which is a version of (CP5), Hacking concludes that the evidence furnishes support for both an hypothesis and its negation. He does not seem to consider this an objection. But as we have seen, for the notion of its being right to increase confidence upon coming to know something, it is impossible that $A R_s B$, and $A R_s \sim B$. It would indeed be rather difficult to imagine any coherent concept of support or confirmation in which it is an acceptable description of our case to say that the evidence supports or confirms that the die will fall six uppermost, and that it will not, and supports or confirms that it will fall five uppermost, and that it will not. So it seems to me that the case not only shows conclusively that (CP5) must be rejected, but casts grave doubt on whether its analogue could be accepted for any notion of support.

The second counterexample to (CP5) is in principle due to Carnap.[6] It consists in the description of a case in which P is a reason for Q, but not a reason for the disjunction Q v T. But since Q entails

[5] Hacking, *The Logic of Statistical Inference*, 1965, p. 33.
[6] Carnap, *The Logical Foundations of Probability*, 1950, p. 386.

the disjunction Q v T, this is again a counterexample to (CP5). The principle of the case is that there exists a total number of possibilities, and if any of some proportion of them is fulfilled, Q is true, and similarly for Q v T. The evidence P restricts the possibilities to a number of which those fulfilling Q constitute a *greater* proportion, while those fulfilling Q v T constitute a *lesser* proportion, than they do of the total. P thus constitutes a reason for Q, and a reason against Q v T. Here is a case which is an instance of this.

I am at a festival where two choirs are singing. The first choir, A, is made up of 10 women and 40 boys. The second, B, is made up of 30 women and no boys, but 20 men. Each choir thus numbers 50, and the total number of singers is 100. Of these, 40 are women, and 40 boys, so the total number of singers who are either women or boys is 80. I know that this is how the singers are distributed. I then hear a voice and, being unmusical, cannot tell whether it is that of a woman or a boy or a man, nor from which choir it came. I simply cannot favour any hypothesis on the basis of what I hear. Still, on the basis of my knowledge of the proportion of singers I may have a stronger or weaker degree of confidence in the various hypotheses. I then come to know that the voice came from choir B. It is then surely right for me to increase my confidence that the singer was a woman: three-fifths of choir B are women, and only two-fifths of the total. But it is right for me to decrease confidence that the singer is a woman or a boy. For three-fifths of choir B are women or boys, but four-fifths of the total. So here we have a substitution instance of $P R_s Q$, $Q \rightarrow Q$ v T, and $\sim(P R_s \ Q$ v $T)$, contrary to (CP5).

Actually Carnap's case is even stronger than this, for in his case the evidence is a reason for *each* of the disjuncts and still a reason against the disjunction. This is because the proportion of possibilities satisfying Q v T in the total is greater than that in the class to which P restricts us, whereas the proportion satisfying Q, *and* the proportion satisfying T are each greater in the class to which P restricts us than in the total. Then Q v T has a better chance of being true before P is taken into consideration, whereas each of Q, and T, have a better chance of being true afterwards. A case which is an instance of this is the following:

There is a chess competition in which New York plays the Strangers. Each team is made up of Senior and Junior players, men and women, as follows:

	New York	*Strangers*
Senior	MM	WWW
Junior	MWW	MM

When the competition is over, I am wondering whether a woman has won (H), or a Stranger has won (K), having absolutely no knowledge about the matter except that the constitution of the teams was as stated. I am then told that a Senior won, (E). Quite clearly this situation is an instance of the description I gave, and:

$$(E\,R_s\,H) \;\&\; (E\,R_s\,K) \;\&\; \sim(E\,R_s\,(H \vee K))$$

again contrary to (CP5).

This case is important, because faced with my choir example, we might be tempted to suppose that if the evidence is a reason for one disjunct, and not a reason against the other, then it will be a reason for the disjunction. But this example of Carnap's refutes that suggestion. Furthermore the principle of the case is such that another suggestion, that if the evidence is a reason for each disjunct, and not a reason against the disjunction, then it must be a reason for the disjunction, can be seen to be untrue. For we could clearly manipulate the proportions so that the evidence is a reason for H, and for K, and is irrelevant to H v K.

It will be seen that in using these examples an important assumption is made, namely that in some way reasons are commensurate with proportions, so that in the situations described, coming to know that a thing is in a class in which a higher proportion of members is ϕ provides a reason for supposing that, or makes it right to increase confidence that, that thing is ϕ. I shall be discussing this assumption in detail in chapter 6. For the present we may just say that it does seem true that in the cases described the evidence makes it right to increase confidence in the way suggested, and these cases are therefore satisfactory counterexamples to (CP5). We may also mention that the following proposal, made by B. A. Brody, does not seem very plausible.[7] Brody suggests that a satisfactory concept of entailment might not have the unrestrictedly valid principle that A entails A v B, so that Carnap's case could be evaded by denying that H entails H v K. But this is quite unacceptable. For although such a proposal has been made as a move towards deny-

[7] Brody, "Confirmation and Explanation", *Journal of Philosophy*, 1968, p. 288.

ing Lewis's first independent proof of the identity of strict implication and entailment,[8] there is little to be said for it. It is perfectly obvious that from the truth of 'a woman has won' there follows as a matter of logic the truth of 'a woman has won v a Stranger has won'; so even if the principle of entailment were not unrestrictedly valid, there would be nothing to be said for supposing that this case fails to obey it.

(*CP6*) This is the principle known as the "converse consequence condition". As I have already mentioned, it cannot be accepted together with (L3) and (CP5). For let T be a proposition to which P is irrelevant, then let Q be a proposition such that $P\,R_s\,Q$. Then by (CP6), $P\,R_s\,(Q\,\&\,T)$, and by (CP5), $P\,R_s\,T$, contrary to supposition. In the presence of (CP5) and (CP6), a proposition which is a reason for any proposition is a reason for every proposition. However, we have just disproved the universal validity of (CP5), so we cannot use it in arguing the truth or falsity of (CP6).

Nevertheless we can show that (CP6) is false. Consider again the example of the chess match. Suppose again that all I know is the constitution of the teams. Suppose I am interested in whether a New Yorker wins (N) and a Junior wins (J). My evidence this time is that a man wins (E). By the same principle of associating reasons and proportions that we used in discussing (CP5), we see that $(E\,R_s\,N)$, $(E\,R_s\,J)$ and $\sim(E\,R_s\,(N\,\&\,J))$. Yet $(N\,\&\,J)$ entails N, and $(N\,\&\,J)$ entails J. So we have an exception to (CP6).

Again a simpler, but weaker, sort of case can easily be described. Intuitively, what is needed to provide an exception to the converse consequence condition is a case where the reason for supposing that A will happen is a reason against supposing that the conditions which allow the joint truth of (A & B) are satisfied. And again, the surprising thing about Carnap's example is that this can be met without the evidence itself providing a reason against B – on the contrary the evidence is evidence for B.

Another counterexample can easily be adapted from the die case.

---

[8] The first writer to suggest this was Nelson, "Intensional Relations", *Mind*, 1930. He denies that it is unrestrictedly true that A & B entails A, whence by contraposition he would deny that unrestrictedly A entails A v B. Anderson and Belnap, in "Tautological Entailments", *Philosophical Studies*, 1962, do not deny this, but only the corresponding principle for an alleged stronger, intensional, sense of "or".

Suppose A is the hypothesis that the die has been weighted to fall six uppermost, and B the hypothesis that it has been weighted to fall five uppermost. We suppose that both of these could be true of a die, and indeed Marco occasionally puts weights opposite both sides of the dice he makes (so that although they consistenly fall on high numbers, they don't consistently fall on the same high number, thus avoiding suspicion). Luigi on the other hand always weights his dice for one or the other but never both. Then if I don't know which of Luigi and Marco manufactured my die, but I know that one of them did, the evidence E that Luigi manufactured the die is a reason for A, and a reason for B, but a reason against (A & B).

(*CP2*) This is in some ways the most interesting of the entailment principles. For it is a natural thought that if evidence is a reason for an hypothesis, it may be so *in virtue of* the hypothesis entailing the evidence. We shall see that this cannot be so.

It is wise to remove at the outset the case where Q is identical with (P & ∼ P). It is clear that (P & ∼ P) entails P. It is not very inviting to say that $P R (P \& \sim P)$, although the obscurity of the counterfactual clause in this case ('If it had not been certain that P & ∼ P is false, it would have been right to increase confidence in it upon coming to know P') makes its truth or falsity very difficult to establish. I think the best thing, in the absence of a theory of counterfactuals where the fact that is countered is a logical truth, is to hold that it is *not* the case that $P R (P \& \sim P)$. For remembering that 'R' is presented as an analysis of 'reason', surely it is more than misleading to say that every proposition gives a reason for a contradiction; it is false. (CP2) must then be restricted:

(CP2′) $(Q \to P) \& \sim (Q \to \sim P) \to (P R Q)$

Let us consider firstly the case where Q is a conjunction of which P is one of the conjuncts. Q can therefore be represented as P & T, where T is to be consistent with P, i.e., P & T does not entail ∼ P. Then *is* it always right to increase confidence in a conjunction upon coming to know one of the conjuncts?

There is, I think, one important motive for saying that it is. This derives from the connection of 'a reason for an hypothesis' with 'something that increases the probability of an hypothesis'. We have not yet discussed the relation between these notions, and so far we have remained agnostic on the question of whether the logic of '*R*' is such that it can be considered a probability-raising relation. But if '*R*' is to be considered a probability-raising relation, then the truth of (CP2′) must be maintained. The proof of this can be put very simply. (For a similar argument, see W. Todd.)[9] Let us symbolise 'The probability of H upon evidence E' as 'Prob (H, E)'. Suppose the antecedent evidence is A. Then by the multiplication axiom for probability:

$$\text{Prob} \, ((P \, \& \, T), A)$$
$$= \text{Prob} \, (P, A) \qquad \times \text{Prob} \, (T, (P \, \& \, A))$$
$$\text{and Prob} \, ((P \, \& \, T), (P \, \& \, A))$$
$$= \text{Prob} \, (P, (P \, \& \, A)) \quad \times \text{Prob} \, (T, (P \, \& \, (P \, \& \, A)))$$
$$= 1 \qquad\qquad\qquad \times \text{Prob} \, (T, (P \, \& \, A))$$

The second expression is obviously greater than the first if and only if Prob (P, A) is less than 1. For remember that T is not inconsistent with P, nor certainly false. So in any case in which we come to know a previously uncertain P, this raises the probability of any conjunction of which it is a conjunct. So to preserve the connection of reasoning and raising probability we must say that for uncertain (P & T), it is universally true that P *R* (P & T).

This is a very strong argument, but it is important to see how little use it is in furthering the concept of reasoning for an hypothesis. For if this is the argument for accepting P *R* (P & T), then P *R* (P & T) *solely because* P *R* P. For it is *solely because* coming to know P raises the probability of P to 1 that we could conclude that the second figure above must be greater than the first. But then we cannot use this piece of reasoning in aiming for any conclusion other than P – which we already know. For given that we have a reason for the conjunction, still we have no right at all to further our confidence in anything other than the P part of the conjunction: T remains precisely as probable as before. Since this is of the last importance in discussing the notion of reasoning I shall elaborate it in detail.

Suppose we admit that universally P *R* (P & T). Then also, P *R* (P & ~T). But from this we cannot conclude either that P *R* T, or that P *R* ~T, for to conclude either we should conclude both, which is inconsistent by (L2). We have here a breakdown of (CP5). Then in using P *R* (P & T) to enable us to reason for something

[9] Todd, "Probability and the Theory of Confirmation", *Mind*, 1967, p. 260.

going beyond the evidence P, we need a further premiss; namely that P *R* T. Consider for example the case of instantial confirmation of a general law. Suppose the evidence is P, that all observed As are B. Let T be that all unobserved As are B. Then P & T together are identical with the proposition that all As are B. We are assured now that P *R* (P & T). But the rub is that we are equally assured that P *R* (P & ~T): in each case merely because P *R* P. So if we take P to be a reason for the generalisation simply because of this, then we cannot reason from the generalisation to the unobserved: we first have to argue that P *R* T, as opposed to P *R* ~T.

(CP2′) then assures us that 'all smelled roses smell nice' is a reason for 'all smelled roses and all unsmelled ones smell nice', and for 'all smelled roses smell nice and all the rest smell horrible', but just because of this catholicism is useless as a base for expecting anything of an hitherto unsmelled rose. It is then vital to realise that when we use evidence for a generalisation, and the generalisation for prediction, *it cannot be in virtue of* the evidence being entailed by the generalisation that our procedure is rational. It must rather be because of our evidence being itself a reason for the proposition about unobserved instances. This will characteristically happen when the proposition about the unobserved instances states their similarity to the observed instances, but why this should be so is of course part of our original problem.

The plausibility of (CP2′) may have contributed to the idea that the problem of the justification of induction has been superseded by the problem of choosing from amongst various different hypotheses. But if this is to be more than a vacuous restatement of the problem, (CP2′) lends it very little support. For (CP2′) will assure us, it is true, that evidence of observed As being B will be a reason for supposing that all As are B. But this is a pyrrhic victory, for it fails to give us a reason for expecting anything of the unobserved As: it fails to give us a *usable* reason for the generalisation. And it can hardly be claimed that the old problem has been solved, dissolved, or superseded until we know that we do possess such usable reasons.

Conclusion

The other main aspect of the logic of reasoning which bears upon this work is its connection with the raising of probabilities. We probably find it natural to admit (CP2′) and the corresponding distinction between usable and useless reasons for hypotheses. But although there exists formal argument that the logic of reasoning is in some ways distinct from the logic of raising probabilities, we can afford to remain agnostic on this. The question remaining for later discussion is whether the problem of justification is best conducted in terms of raising probabilities.

The situation at present is that we have established a good deal about the concept of a reason. We have closely identified the problem of justification and described the purpose which good reasoning must serve. The logic of the notion is certainly worthy of further investigation, but in this chapter we have simply separated out various invalid principles which might easily be thought to hold. In particular we have exposed the inadequacy of the view that evidence is a reason for a conclusion in virtue of the conclusion entailing the evidence – this gives us no way of reasoning which entitles us to confidence in anything beyond our evidence. So if our evidence is to give a usable reason for a conclusion, then it must bear some more substantive relation to it than any we have yet identified. To investigate this we need a firm grasp of the resemblances for which we do reason. So to step further we now need to look at the other major concept involved in setting up the problem, the concept of a resemblance or similarity. When we have done that we shall be in a much better position to estimate the adequacy of most approaches to the problem, and in a much better position to see where to turn for a solution.

4
Goodman's paradox

How it arises

I have now said a great deal about the notion of a reason. But the other part of the problem is the notion of the resemblances or similarities for which we reason, and this concept we have so far neglected. It is, it is true, difficult to maintain any sense of direction in the avalanche of questions which is released if we unsettle this concept: do we reason for any similarity; just some; how do we select; is this a matter of our experience, perceptions, language, logic; what is it for two things to be similar in some respect anyhow? Fortunately the questions important to our enquiry answer themselves in an orderly fashion if we concentrate upon a particularly forceful and precise way of putting disquiet about the notion of a similarity, namely, Goodman's paradox. This procedure has two additional advantages. At its conclusion we shall understand much better what sort of contribution the formal theory of probability could make to our problem. We shall also understand much better what is wrong with a number of important theories of rational belief.

We saw in the first chapter that two sorts of case of using induction are naturally distinguished. The evidence considered may state that some of a kind of thing have a feature F, the conclusion being that some or all others of that kind of thing are F; or the evidence may concern just one thing, stating that it has been F at certain times, the conclusion being that the thing in question will be F at some or all other times.

In terms of the first sort of case Goodman constructs his paradox by attempting to produce a predicate having the following three properties:

1. The predicate is properly used to express a property G which relates to a property F which some of a class of things can be known to possess, in such a way that if those things are F, then they are also G.

2. *G* and *F* are apparently symmetrical with respect to inductive reasoning. That is, if some of a class of things being *F* is a reason for supposing other members of the class to be *F*, then some of a class of things being *G* is just as good a reason for supposing other members to be *G*.

3. The supposition that some unobserved things of a class are *G* is inconsistent with the supposition that they are *F*.

It is further clear that if Goodman can produce one such predicate, then for any *F* he can produce any number of such predicates, giving any number of apparently equally reasonable but mutually inconsistent predictions about the properties of unobserved members of a class. This is paradoxical because it conflicts with the apparently necessarily true proposition that some such predictions are better supported by given evidence than others.[1]

In terms of the second sort of case the paradox would be constructed by producing a property *G*, relating to a property *F* which a thing can be known to have possessed at given times, such that if it was *G* at those times then it was *F* at those times. *G* and *F* are similarly symmetrical with respect to confirmation, and the prediction that the thing will be *G* at some given times is inconsistent with the prediction that it will be *F* at those times.

In addition to setting up the paradox, however, Goodman also advances a solution to it. His solution is to deny that for the predicates he advances condition 2 is satisfied, on the ground that these predicates are not so "well-entrenched" as others. A predicate is entrenched in proportion to the number of occasions on which it has been the hero of a successful prediction: the more times it has been successfully predicted that what it expresses will be true of an object at a later time, the better entrenched the predicate. This

---

[1] People sometimes stop here, and express the view that Goodman has done nothing more than rediscover the old point that there can be a problem of choice of which hypothesis is confirmed by observations. This is totally inaccurate, for two reasons. Firstly he provides a mechanical way of making quite outrageously different hypotheses seem to be confirmed by any observation. Secondly he advances a powerful argument against any attempt to rectify this by appealing to a notion of a similarity, and himself attempts to show that the only anchorage in his sea of hypotheses is given by the history of the language. In discussing this second claim one is involved in matters raised in none of the literature preceding the paradox.

solution does not seem at all plausible, and it is necessary to the purpose of this chapter to show that the arguments in favour of it are inadequate, and to show what is the correct solution.

Clearly the success of Goodman's endeavour depends upon his ability to produce such a paradoxical property, and upon his ability to establish his own solution. His own exposition introduces the predicate as follows, t being a variable ranging over times:

> "Now let me introduce another predicate less familiar than 'green'. It is the predicate 'grue' and it applies to all things examined before t just in case they are green but to other things just in case they are blue."[2]

I think we can only properly take this introduction to mean that the predicate expresses what may otherwise be expressed by a truth-functional disjunction with the notion of 'being examined' involved: *grue*: a thing is grue if and only if *either* the thing has been examined before t and is green, *or* the thing has not been so examined, and is blue.

It is usual to let t be some arbitrary time in the future, say midnight on the last day of 1985, and I shall call this value T; and it is usual to take emeralds as the class of things about which we are concerned to predict the grueness or greenness. It is worthwhile pointing out that if we let t be some time in the past no paradox arises. Some emeralds, namely those discovered and examined for colour before whatever time it was, are grue; those found since are not, unless, of course, they are blue. It is also clear that if t did take some value in the past, upon being presented with a green emerald I could *not* determine whether it is grue, for to tell this I would have to know whether it was examined before the fatal date. Only if it was does it satisfy both conditions of the first disjunct. The importance of this point will emerge in due course.

There is no doubt that "grue" so defined satisfies the first and third conditions upon the paradoxical predicate. For consider all the emeralds which we have examined and know thereby to be green. Now we may be slightly unhappy about saying that we have therefore observed them to be grue, i.e. observed them to be examined before T and green, or not so examined and blue, but they certainly *are* grue, for they satisfy the first disjunct, and, having observed them and seen that they are green, and knowing that the

[2] Goodman, *Fact, Fiction, and Forecast*, 1955, ch. III, § 4, p. 74.

time is before T, we can properly claim to know that they are grue. Consider also the prediction that some unexamined emeralds are grue: given that among these there are emeralds which come to be examined only after T, and therefore do not satisfy the first disjunct, we must conclude that they satisfy the second. That is, the prediction that emeralds not examined by T are grue entails the prediction that they are blue, and is inconsistent with the prediction that they are green.

A primitive solution

Any solution to the paradox with this predicate must therefore show that the second condition is not satisfied, that is, it must show that knowledge that some things of a class are grue is not a good reason for supposing that all other things of that class are grue, or for supposing that members of the class which are to be examined after a certain time will be grue. And indeed, it does appear plausible to suppose that such knowledge is not a good reason for such a prediction. For if we look at the definition of "grue" it would appear that such knowledge is not a reason for such a prediction because the property *differentiates* between examined and unexamined emeralds, so that to make such a prediction is to expect a difference between some emeralds including those which we have examined, and others, and to expect such a difference appears to be exactly what the justification of induction tries to show to be unreasonable. It therefore appears that Goodman's problem simply reduces to the original problem, which he has simply put in a rather different form. I believe that this reaction can be shown to be the right one, although a great deal must be said to defend it from Goodman's objections.

Let us firstly consider a situation in which it is reasonable to suppose that emeralds examined after T will be grue. Because of some belief a group of emerald miners always treats emeralds in a certain way before bringing them into the light of day; they believe that this serves some purpose but do not believe that it alters the colour of the gems. An enquiring miner knows that all emeralds are green by the time that they are examined, and he knows that the practice of treating the gems will cease at midnight on the last day of 1985: the government has made this regulation. But he wonders what colour emeralds are before being treated, being dissatisfied with the prevalent belief that the treatment does not alter their colour, and to form an estimate he treats a sapphire in the same way, and the sapphire turns green, indeed many blue things turn green under the operation, and most green things turn some other colour. The miner now rationally believes:

  (i) All emeralds examined before T are green.
 (ii) If they had not been so examined, they would have been blue.
(iii) All emeralds are either observed before T and green, or not observed before T and blue.

In fact the miner is wrong about the colour of undiscovered emeralds, but he has rationally come to believe that all emeralds are grue, and the basis for this judgement is his belief in (i) and (ii). Now we might certainly believe (i), so we seem to differ from the miner in not believing (ii). A fair characterisation of this difference is that he has reason to suppose that something occurs which *distinguishes* the colour of those emeralds examined before T from that of those emeralds which are not, and we do not.

The story shows that it is possible to describe a situation in which coming to know that all hitherto examined emeralds are grue ought to increase one's confidence that all emeralds are grue. If the miner knows that things which are blue tend to turn green under the treatment, and that things which are green tend to turn some other colour, and also knows that all examined emeralds will have been previously treated, and that the time is before T, then coming to know that all hitherto examined emeralds are grue ought to increase his confidence that all emeralds are grue, i.e. that the ones examined before T will be found to be green, and those not examined before T will be blue. Of course, this has nothing to do with the relative entrenchments of "green" and "grue" in the man's language – nothing in my story demands that the miner is not English-speaking – it is just that he is in the unusual but not unknown situation in which it is reasonable to believe that the conditions of observation affect the property observed.

The primitive objection to using the fact that examined things are grue as a reason for supposing that all things of some sort are grue is not just that grueness somehow involves a reference to a point in space or time: more important is the serious defect that it uses this reference to segregate emeralds including those which we have examined from those which we have not, but about which we are predicting. This will become clearer when we have considered the argument which Goodman would use against this approach. For Goodman would certainly object that whether or not we think that a predicate does differentiate some members of a class from others, so that we cannot normally inductively use the fact that some members of a class possess the property it expresses as a reason for supposing the others to do so, is itself a matter of the entrenchment of the predicate within the language. In other words, he would claim that nothing I could say about there being a difference between examined emeralds being grue and unexamined ones being grue could provide an alternative account to his, which depends upon the fact that we have not used the word "grue" very often to make successful predictions.

It will be seen immediately that this makes a great difference to any conception of the problem of induction. For we try to justify making the prediction that the next emerald we come across will be green on the basis that others we have examined are. Goodman claims that we only find this a similarity between the next emerald and the previous ones because of the past history of the word "green" in our language. There is no deep reason for this word to have had such a successful history, when "grue" was used so scantily, but its having had such a history is all that can explain our propensity to think of the next green emerald as similar to the previous ones, and to expect the next one to be green like the previous ones. If "grue" had been the predicate used in many successful predictions, we would find it natural to think of a future blue emerald as similar to the previously examined green ones (supposing t to take the present as its value), and would predict that the next emerald would be blue. Clearly if this nominalism is correct many are going to feel that such a historical explanation of why we make the predictions that we do does nothing to justify them against their rivals. According to Goodman's argument our preference for one prediction is based purely on history, not on any likelihood of its being true. So we must now scrutinise the argument which Goodman advances.

Goodman's argument is very simple. He points out that we can define another new predicate "bleen" in exactly the same way as we define "grue" but substituting "green" for "blue" and vice versa throughout. Thus a thing is bleen if and only if either the thing has been examined before t and is blue, or the thing has not been so examined and is green. It is then possible to "define" blueness and greenness in terms of grueness and bleenness: *blue*: a thing is blue if and only if *either* the thing has been examined before t and is bleen, *or* has not been examined before t, and is grue.

Similarly for "green" with "bleen" and "grue" reversed. I think it can be seen that with these two predicates in the uses described for them, this does give a "definition" of blueness. For the disjuncts expand upon substituting the original definitions of "grue" and "bleen" to give: 'a thing is blue if and only if *either* the thing has been examined before t and (has been examined before t and is blue or has not been so examined and is green) *or* the thing has not been examined before t and (has been examined before t and is green or has not been so examined and is blue)'. And it is true that a thing is blue if and only if this is satisfied. I mention this because it is not obvious that there is this interdefinability, and indeed with some predicates which people have taken Goodman to be talking about, it does not obtain.

Having established interdefinability of "grue" and "bleen" with "blue" and "green" Goodman continues (p. 79):

> "But equally truly, if we start with 'grue' and 'bleen', then 'blue' and 'green' will be explained in terms of 'grue' and 'bleen' and a temporal term. . .Thus qualitativeness is an entirely relative matter and does not by itself establish any dichotomy of predicates. This relativity seems to be completely overlooked by those who contend that the qualitative character of a predicate is a criterion for its good behaviour."

And I think there is no doubt that he would use the same argument against my attempt to show that his paradoxical predicates really do differentiate between examined and unexamined emeralds. But is this argument really sufficient to show that qualitativeness, or differentiation, is an entirely relative matter?

Logic and language

The interdefinability does show that *if* we are familiar with the uses of "grue" and "bleen" we can *describe* the uses of "blue" and "green" in terms of them and conjunction, disjunction, and a temporal term, and "examined". It does not show that this could

be an explanation of the uses of "blue" and "green", because it
does not show that anybody could be familiar with the uses of the
paradoxical predicates without being familiar with the uses of
"blue" and "green" to begin with. So there is an incompleteness
in this argument of Goodman's right at the beginning. But Goodman might claim that somebody could use "grue" and "bleen"
correctly without being able to use "blue" or "green" or any
synonyms, and even although the interdefinability does not show
this, it would be difficult to establish that it is impossible. However
there is a more important point. For there is an asymmetry to which
the interdefinability is completely irrelevant. I shall present it first
as a simple brute fact about human beings. This is that you could
not tell that a thing is grue without *either* examining it *and* knowing
whether it is before or after midnight on the last day of 1985, *or*
knowing whether or not it was examined before that time. Suppose
for example that I am examining emeralds, I cannot tell, just by
looking at them, whether they are grue, because I cannot tell, just
by looking at them, what time it is or at what time they were first
examined. If we really ponder a moment the predicate "grue",
defined on p. 63 above, and what we need to tell to find out whether
either disjunct is true, this should be quite obvious. The epistemological point is perhaps clearer if we consider someone presented
with a tray of green emeralds at some time after the end of 1985: he
cannot tell which ones are grue without knowing which ones were
found and examined before the end of 1985, and therefore satisfy
the first disjunct in terms of which "grue" is defined.

I pointed out above that the interdefinability does not by itself
show that there could be a language in which "grue" and "bleen",
in their described uses, are primitive, with the uses of "blue" and
"green" *explained* in terms of them. But even the further claim
that there could be such a language is not enough to show that
it is a language-relative matter whether or not a predicate in a
certain use differentiates examined from unexamined objects. For in
pointing out that knowing whether a thing is grue involves knowing
facts about the time at which it was first examined,[3] I am not
contradicted by someone stating that "grue" could be a *primitive*
predicate in its described use, but only by someone claiming that it

---

[3] Apart from knowing by relying on someone else's report or other
reliable sign. It is what is involved in *telling* that a thing is grue that is
vital.

could be an *observation* predicate in its described use, where an observation predicate is at least one whose application does not involve knowledge of the time, or of whether or not the thing to which it is applied was examined before a certain time. I think it should be fairly clear that no facts about interdefinability have the slightest relevance to showing that "grue" and "bleen" could be observation predicates in this sense.

We are already then a long way beyond the history of the language. "Grue" in its described use differs from "green" not only in its history, but also in its epistemology. We cannot tell whether a thing with which we are confronted is grue unless we know the time at which it was examined first. We can tell that a thing with which we are confronted is green without knowing that fact about it. The word "grue" could have been used throughout all creation without altering that difference one jot. However, it may still look as though we are left with a point about human beings, and what we can tell with our sensory apparatus. So although we are beyond relativising a resemblance and the rationality of a prediction to a language, we may yet need to relativise it to a particular sensory apparatus. But in fact even this gains no support from the existence of Goodman's predicate, since we can show that it differs logically from its rival "green".

For it can be proved that there is a logical asymmetry between grueness and similar properties on the one hand, and blueness and similar properties on the other. The logical asymmetry is that to tell that something is grue *entails* telling not only what it looks like, but also what time it is, or at what time it was first examined, whereas telling that something is blue does not entail telling either of these things. Furthermore no facts about how grueness or blueness is expressed in a particular language alter this asymmetry. Nor do facts about the possibility of people having extraordinary sensory faculties. The asymmetry upon which the solution of the paradox depends is *not* a psychological one, it is not one which depends upon any contingent fact about the way in which we, with our sensory abilities, find it natural to classify things. For I am not denying that there could be a people who can tell immediately, at any time, whether something with which they are presented is grue. We cannot do this, but we can consistently imagine someone, perhaps with some extraordinary sensory faculty, who could at any time state correctly whether a thing is grue or not, and apparently just by looking at it. What I am denying is that anyone could do this without equally being able to tell, just by looking at the thing, whether or not it was examined before the end of 1985, or whether or not the time is before or after the end of 1985.

We can, for example, imagine somebody who appears to use the word "grue" in the way described, and who is mining emeralds throughout New Year's Eve, 1985. He correctly says, as he turns up green ones and examines them, "Ah, these are grue", until at midnight he turns up a green one and says, "Funny, here is one which is not grue." But now suppose that we ask him the time, and he says that he doesn't know if it has passed midnight, and we ask him if anyone had ever previously dug up that emerald, examined it for colour, and replaced it in the ground, and he says he doesn't know that either. We have, it seems to me, *conclusive* evidence that he didn't know that the emerald was not grue, so that either he was not using the word "grue" in accordance with the description we gave of its meaning, or he was mistakenly claiming knowledge.

The possibility that possession of a property by examined members of a class is a different matter from possession of it by unexamined ones is determined by other conditions than the length of the predicate expressing that property, or the overtness of occurrance of words like "examined" or "midnight on the last day of 1985" in that predicate. These other conditions refer to the use of the predicate, in particular to what we must know to know that what it expresses is true of a given object. These logical conditions are obviously not functions of the linguistic form of the predicate ("grue" is as short as "blue") nor of the length of time for which it has been used. To take a parallel case. There could, I imagine, be a language in which the words "squabble", "squot", and "blot" are primitive, with the following uses:

squabble: a thing is squabble if and only if it is both square and blue.
squot: a thing is squot if and only if it is square and not blue.
blot: a thing is blot if and only if it is blue and not square.

We can fairly easily imagine children being taught the use, or at least the application, of these words, before knowing any synonyms of "square" and "blue"; they would later learn that a thing is square if and only if it is squabble or squot, and blue if and only if it is squabble or blot. But this does not show that these children could recognise that something is squabble without recognising that it is square or without knowing its colour; it is simply irrelevant to the logical fact that you cannot know that something is square and blue without knowing that it is square.

But this is a logical truth (although of course the corresponding general principle 'If P entails Q, knowing P entails knowing Q' is not universally true) and it is the existence of logical truths of this form which is the lynch-pin of the solution. If we doubt this logical truth in the case of the children, we can ask ourselves how we would try to determine that they know that something is squabble, as opposed to knowing that it possesses some contingently co-extensive property. The only possibility appears to be to show that they attribute squabbleness on the basis firstly of shape and secondly of colour. The point is really just an application of the familiar distinction between intension and extension. We are all aware that using a word with a given extension does not entail using it with a particular corresponding intension. What we have added to this is that if someone uses a word "grue" as extensionally equivalent to the word in Goodman's sense, and finds it natural to classify early green and late blue emeralds together, still not only need we not attribute Goodman's sense to his word, but we are positively disallowed from doing so unless the logic of his word is right; unless, that is, knowledge of whether it is grue in his sense entails knowledge of when it was first examined, i.e., knowledge of at least one of two disjuncts, whose conjunction defines "grue".[4]

This conclusively refutes the supposition that interdefinability shows symmetry in everything but frequency of occurrence; in particular it refutes the idea that whether or not a predicate expresses something differentiating between examined and unexamined members of a class is a matter of its frequency of occurrence, and *must* be a matter of something like that because of interdefinability. However, I expect it will be felt that there remains some point to the paradox, and that I have not yet presented a solution of it. I have so far claimed that grueness differentiates between examined

---

[4] It has been suggested by Dr Hacking in a paper read to the B.S.P.S. in September 1970 that an extensional version of the paradox can be generated. The point would be that if a paradox can be generated by using predicates which do not have the warped epistemology of "grue", then it would be immune to my solution. I discuss this further below, p. 80.

and unexamined emeralds in a way in which greenness doesn't, that this is shown by considering what it is to know that a thing is grue, and that these epistemological asymmetries are not simply language-relative, nor simply psychological. I can say nothing more about the last point, but I shall try to explain the first a little more, and explain in what way it leads to a reduction of the paradox to the original problem.

Suppose someone said: "It is all very well claiming that the prediction that all emeralds are grue differentiates those emeralds examined before a certain time from the rest, in respect of colour. Why should this matter? After all, the prediction that all emeralds are green differentiates those examined before a certain time from the rest, in respect of grueness. So this description does nothing to distinguish one prediction from the other in irrationality, given the evidence from examined emeralds." We must, I think, only remember the logical asymmetries to realise that there are differentiations and differentiations, and that it might be quite possible to separate them in point of irrationality. After all, a man who treats all men equally well segregates those whom he has seen, and (seen and treated well or not seen and treated badly) from those whom he has not seen, and (seen and treated badly or not seen and treated well) but he is not a segregationist for all that. If we call the expression in the first bracket "A" and the expression in the second "B", then he is not exercising prejudice in treating men he has seen in way A and men he has not in way B, for to do this would be to treat all men equally, however often we were to use the expressions A and B or any shorter synonymous expressions.

This point is worth developing a little, to demonstrate how easy it is to fake an appearance of a change or a similarity once we allow ourselves to use Goodman's device. We can imagine a country (or perhaps just describe one) where judges treat poor men unkindly and rich men kindly. Perhaps this practice offends against a particular judge's egalitarian instincts. But, we can assure him, it need not do so. For let us say that a judge treats a person x *pitchly* if and only if, either x is poor and the judge treats him unkindly, or x is rich and the judge treats him kindly. And similarly a judge treats a person x *roorly* if and only if, either x is poor and the judge treats him kindly, or x is rich and the judge treats him unkindly. Now our imaginary judge treats all men alike: he treats them pitchly. It is true, we concede, that this involves treating some kindly and others unkindly, but then treating all men equally kindly would involve treating some pitchly and others roorly. So he need have no worse a conscience than the justest of egalitarians. We might even add that any residual feeling that the judge is being inegalitarian springs from the fact that the words "kind" and "unkind" have a more established history than my new words "pitch" and "roor". It would be strange to pick on their predictive successes, when the case has nothing to do with prediction. But we could find some fact in the history of the relevant pairs; and if history started to go the way of my new pair, which would be a wonderful convenience in some circumstances, treating poor men unkindly and rich men kindly would be the only egalitarian thing to do.

It is a little noticed fact that Goodman's method, since it raises a general question about the concept of a similarity, provides problems in fields other than that of prediction. Now why might a judge want to say that treating all men pitchly is not really treating them all alike? The answer is obvious. Treating all men pitchly is not treating them all alike, because you must know whether a man is rich or poor before you know how to treat him. If a defendant comes before you then you must know the state of his pocket before you know whether to put him in prison or set him free. And that simple epistemological fact shows that treating all men pitchly is not treating them all alike: it is using the state of their finances to determine their treatment, and that is inegalitarian.

Similarly with grueness. To know whether a thing is grue entails knowing whether it was examined before T, and had one feature, or was not, and had another. To know whether a thing is green does not entail knowing whether it was examined at any time at all. So differentiating things examined before T from others in point of grueness is not differentiating at all, whereas doing the same in respect of greenness must be.

It may of course still be asked why it is irrational to expect a difference between things examined before a certain time and others, but here the true nature of the "new riddle of induction", and its importance for our enquiry, is revealed. For once we have established that Goodman's predicate really does distinguish between those of a class including those we have observed, and the rest of that class, it is apparent that nothing more needs to be done to establish the irrationality of believing that it applies to all members of a class, than needs to be done to establish the rationality of induction. That is, suppose that I know something non-differentiating (by the epistemological criteria) to be true of all examined members of a class of things. You form the corresponding Goodman predicate, parallel to "grue", for some value of t. I can establish that you are differentiating between instances examined before T and those which are not, in a way in which I am not. But then, in believing that all members of the class have the Goodman property you are simply postulating a difference between some of the things, including those examined, and others. If, unlike the emerald miner whom I considered, you have no reason for this difference, your prediction is irrational, but its irrationality simply follows from its being rational to expect the future to be like the past. But establishing this is the old riddle of induction, not a new one. In other words, Goodman makes it look as though there is *no* problem of justifying taking the future to be like the past, but there *is* a problem of choosing between the different respects (grueness, greenness) in which the future may be like the past. However, this is wrong, because this new problem reduces to the old problem.

I think this disposes of Goodman's paradox in the form in which he presents it, and disposes of it without relying upon the frequency of occurrence of different predicates in a given language. I do not claim to have shown that the second condition upon the paradoxical predicate is *not* satisfied, but I have shown that to demonstrate that it is satisfied is no other problem than demonstrating the rationality of induction. That is, suppose that I wonder why, in general, observed things of a type all having a property is a reason for unobserved things of that type having it, and you point out the existence of a property, or indeed of many properties, which the observed things possess, but such that, if the unobserved things possess them, then they differ from the observed things. I need do nothing more to show that it is irrational to expect the unobserved things to possess these properties than I need do to show that it is irrational to expect the unobserved things to differ from the observed: but this is the rationality of taking the observed as a guide to the unobserved. The concept of a resemblance is, it appears, free from the historical or psychological arbitrariness which looked like being such a comfort to a sceptic about inductive reasoning.

Another form of the paradox

It will be seen that so far we have only discussed the paradox as it arises for my first sort of case (p. 61). So for completeness we need to say something about the problem as it arises for the second kind of inductive prediction, where we are dealing with the continued possession of a property by one object, rather than with possession of the same property by as yet unexamined members of a class. It is important to describe the property carefully, and a disappointing proportion of the literature on this problem is ostensibly concerned with predicates which in fact fail to satisfy the conditions necessary for the appearance of a paradox (p. 61).[5] Here then is an example which raises the same issues for predictions that an object will remain the same in some respect:

con: At any time t a thing x is a con at t if and only if either (t $<$ T & x is a cow) or (t $>$ T & x is a don)
dow: At any time t a thing x is a dow at t if and only if either (t $<$ T & x is a don) or (t $>$ T & x is a cow)

It can easily be verified that these form a pair like Goodman's own examples, and providing a paradox for the prediction that something, now a cow, will not be a don after the end of 1985, or for the prediction that something, now a don, will not become a cow after the end of 1985. For if a thing which is now a con remains a con after that date, it becomes a don, and if something which is now a dow remains a dow, it becomes a cow. This we are inclined to think of as a change, and expect not to happen. But again, interdefinability of the pair "don" and "cow" in terms of the pair "con" and "dow", the concepts of the end of 1985, temporal order and the truth functions, obtains as with Goodman's example. Again, we could pose the question of what basis exists for predicting that I will be a don and not a dow in 1986. Why expect change in dow-hood rather than change in don-hood?

Again, of course, the answer is that the "change in dow-hood" which comes about through remaining a don is simply a faked appearance of a change. We start the proof of this by pointing out

[5] Examples are discussed in my paper, "Goodman's Paradox", in *Studies in the Philosophy of Science*, ed. Rescher, 1969.

that we wouldn't be able to tell whether a thing remains a dow over a period of time without knowing whether the end of 1985 occurs within that period. For of course, if the thing is a don, and stays a don throughout the period, it will no longer be a dow in the interval between the end of 1985 and the end of the period. Being a dow then entails being a cow. Or if the thing, being a don, miraculously changes into a cow, then unless we can tell that this happens just at the end of 1985, then for all we know it may have forfeited its dow-hood for a certain period. At least for human beings, therefore, the epistemology of telling that something remains a dow is the epistemology of determining that a change happens at the right time. Furthermore, even if exception is taken to the next stage of the argument, we must notice that this is already a long way beyond entrenchment. Because there is no ghost of an appearance that these features of dow-hood arise because of a fact about our language. Suppose the word "dow" to have been used to make good predictions for as long as we like, and it creates no ability to tell whether something remains a dow during the winter of 1985–6, without telling whether it changed into a cow on New Year's Eve. The word "dow" could easily have been used, defined as we have defined it, to make true predictions ever since universities began. For until recently propositions like 'John will become a don' or 'Dons will receive more pay' would have been true if and only if the corresponding proposition 'John will become a dow' or 'Dows will receive more pay' were true. But imagine that it had been so used, and then ask how someone familiar with this use is any better placed than we are to tell whether something remains a dow over the relevant winter. In exactly the same way that we need to know the date, so does he, and whatever the history of the word may have been, if he loses his diary and has no record of the date, he cannot tell that the thing remains a dow.

The next point which I need to establish is that these things are not merely facts about ourselves, but logically necessary truths. For now that entrenchment is shown not to be important, many theorists will say that Goodman has succeeded in relativising rational prediction to the possession of a certain epistemological ability, which it is contingent that we possess. But this too is incorrect. I shall secure this claim by introducing another necessity, which will appear less controversial.

It is logically impossible to tell whether an explosion occurs at midnight without knowing when it is midnight. A certain weight is here put upon "tell". One might, I think, know that an explosion occurs at midnight, because of some reliable sign that it does – such as someone saying that it does, or because of some theoretical connection between the occurrence of the explosion at midnight and some other phenomenon. In such a case one needn't know the time. But equally such cases are in an obvious sense secondary, for the question of the reliability of the sign is only settled by seeing whether the explosion occurs at midnight, and it is that which entails knowledge of the time. This is the sense in which I am, throughout, using "telling".

If it is contingent that we cannot tell whether an explosion occurs at midnight without knowing when it is midnight, what sort of sensory ability or other feature could we gain to free us of this requirement? Of course someone might have abilities which we have not: he may have better eyesight, hearing, detect rumblings and smells which we cannot, even tell the time using sensations which don't help us, like those of heat and cold. But this sort of person simply tells when the explosion occurs by using his own peculiar method of telling when it is midnight. He does not tell whether the explosion occurs at midnight without knowing when it is midnight. So the possibility of that sort of super-sensed being is irrelevant. And I cannot see in what other direction we could possibly search for a relevant extension of our abilities. To put the point another way, it is impossible to describe coming across someone who can tell whether an explosion occurs at midnight without knowing when it is midnight. Again, it is only possible to describe people who, being right about when the explosion occurs, have peculiar methods of telling when it is midnight (or perhaps no method at all; perhaps they know the time without following a method – they're just always right about it).

I incline, therefore, to think that it is logically impossible to tell whether an explosion occurs at midnight without knowing when it is midnight. This by itself solves a class of Goodman cases. For we can form predicates as follows. A night is *e-silent* if and only if at any time t, if t is before or after midnight no explosion occurs, and if t is midnight an explosion occurs. And *e-noisy* if the reverse is the case. These form a pair in just the same way as grue and bleen, or dow and con, and any points that Goodman makes with his original example could be made with these. But none of these points, arising out of the interdefinabilities, or the possibility of what Good-man calls "starting with" the unnatural predicates, is of the least relevance to showing that it is logically possible to tell whether a night is e-silent unless you can tell whether it is midnight.

It is, I hope, by now clear that the same points apply to the con and dow case. Retaining dow-hood is a faked appearance of a similarity because telling that a thing retains dow-hood entails telling that a change happens at the right time, and the fact that this is an entailment shows that this does not depend upon our language or our psychology. And again, the problem of choice between expecting someone to continue a don, and expecting him to continue a dow, after the end of 1985, reduces to the old problem of justifying an expectation of similarity.

Further considerations

Although the solution of Goodman's paradox is now complete, there are certain further aspects of it which it is interesting to mention. People often suppose that the paradox raises some issue concerned with our perception of change and that this is left obscure by all I have said so far. It is often felt too that there is a connection with certain of Wittgenstein's remarks about the possibility of people continuing series in odd ways. I shall therefore try to say a little about the interesting possibilities, again using the con and dow example, whose principal virtue is that the differences between a don and a cow matter to us in a way in which the differences between two colours often do not. Also, since we are less familiar with people who confuse dons with cows than we are with people who confuse colours, the various possibilities may present themselves more forcibly, and the differences between them stand out in sharper relief.

The first possibility is that there could exist a person or persons who just fail to perceive any difference between dons and cows. So they would not perceive a change if they perceived a don chang-ing into a cow, or vice versa. We might speculate about the extent of the sensory disability necessary for someone to be in such an unfortunate state – the extent to which he has to be insensitive to differences of weight, size, shape, sound, touch, smell — but the pos-sibility of someone blind in this way has no relevance to rational prediction. The same is true of the different possibility that someone should be generally able to discriminate between dons and cows, but wouldn't perceive the change if a don turned into a cow at the end of 1985. Neither permanent nor temporary sensory derangement is relevant to Goodman's problem.

Secondly we might suppose that someone could exist who perceives what we do but does not think of the change from a don to a cow as a change. This may be because he has a poor memory. If, for example, I am sitting next to him at dinner, and gradually turn into a cow, he may at each moment think of me as presenting the same appearance as I did at the previous moment, because of his bad memory. But if he remembers how I was, and perceives what is going on, it is difficult to give any sense to saying that he doesn't think of it as *a* change. He may not think of it as an important or surprising change. Similarly someone listening during a silence may hear a bang, and not think of it as an important or surprising event, but what could be meant by saying that he doesn't even think of it as an event at all? A similar point might be made in response to one remark which Wittgenstein imagines his deviant pupil to make.[6] The pupil adds 2 to numbers before 1000 and 4 to numbers after 1000, and on being challenged says "But I went on in the same way." However, if we take an applied example, it is difficult to imagine the pupil saying just this. He is ordered to add bricks two at a time to a pile, and then after he has made a pile of 1000, he suddenly starts adding them four at a time. Unless he suffers from a sudden failure of memory or perception, he will realise that the operation is different: he needs perhaps a bigger hod, two hands, help on the ladder and so on. If his memory and perception are in order the pupil must at least recognise that what he calls "going on in the same way" involves a different and harder physical operation. Again it is not at all clear how someone with adequate awareness of what he is doing could think of himself as going on in exactly the same way.

He may however still think of himself as "going on in the same way" because he has grasped or imagined a similarity compared with which the fact that he is now adding more bricks at a time is unimportant. And this brings us to a second and completely different class of possibilities. Instead of people who are insensitive to a change of which we are aware we now consider people who are

---

[6] Wittgenstein, *Philosophical Investigations*, 1953, § 185.

sensitive to a similarity of which we are not. We may expect something to stay the same in respect of F. Someone else may expect it to
stay the same in respect of G, and also hold the view that if it remains the same in respect of G, it will change in respect of F. It will
be clear that this second view is in effect the belief that G is co-
extensive with some Goodman predicate which could be formed
from F. But G may be a genuine similarity for all that, and there
can in such cases be an interesting conflict of predictions. I shall
present a simple example to make clear the way this sort of possibility relates to Goodman's paradox.

Let us suppose that, as a don, I am an object of concern to civil
servant X, who is attached to the Ministry of Education. I expect
to remain a don after the end of 1985. But someone knows that at
the end of 1985 the civil servant X is to transfer to deal exclusively
with cows for the Ministry of Agriculture. We are then faced with
a choice: either I remain a don and cease to be an object of concern
to X, or I remain an object of concern to X and change from being
a don to a cow. There is an *extensional* connection with the Goodman predicate dow, for at any time a thing is of concern to X if and
only if it is a dow at that time. The two predicates always apply to
just the same things. But it is quite clear which choice should be
made, for it is very common for things to cease to be objects of
concern to civil servants who change Ministries, and very uncommon indeed for dons to become bovine in every respect. So given
that we can find a reason for trusting induction, we can solve the
problem of choice which the example poses.

This is not to say that when such a choice arises there will always
be a clear solution, nor that the criteria of choice will themselves
always be obvious. Suppose for example that we observe certain
ducks and find that they are brown in England. We expect to find
similar ducks in the Arctic, so should we expect them to resemble
English ducks in being brown, or resemble them in being the same
colour as their environment? Either prediction involves one point of
similarity and one of difference. Again, we may have straightforward evidence of what is usual in the way of colour variance in
ducks, or birds, or animals in general. Or we may have a theory
connecting, say, the cause of the brown colour with an item in
English but not Arctic soils. Or there may be no real weight of
evidence on one side or the other. But in any event, the choice
is a real one, and although it creates a problem it creates no para-

dox. For these cases differ from the paradoxical ones precisely in that here either choice involves expecting some similarity, whereas when we oppose a "grue" type of prediction to a normal one, the former involves no expectation of similarity.

Equally, there is no mechanical way of creating these interesting problems of choice. Although predicates like "dow" can be manufactured at will, there is no knowledge which can be brought to bear to create a problem of choosing whether to predict that I will remain the same in respect of being a don, or in some other respect which will involve my changing into a cow. To create such a problem we must satisfy two conditions. We must find a property which I possess and which it is extremely unlikely that I should cease to possess. And we must have excellent reason to suppose that I can continue to possess it after the end of 1985 only by becoming a cow. "Dow" of course fails to satisfy the first condition, since, given that we can solve the problem of induction, there is every likelihood that one will cease to be a dow at the end of 1985, and only the appearance of reason to the contrary. A scientist might come up with such a property but it is hardly probable. This does however indicate the way to a familiar type of sceptical move. For whenever we expect a similarity a sceptic can claim that it is logically possible that there should exist another property which it is more likely that the object should retain, and whose retention would, contingently, involve change in the respect which interests us. But this is of no fundamental interest, since it simply fills out the possibility from which the problem of induction starts, namely that our expectations should be disappointed. It simply adds that it is logically possible that we should be wrong because the object continues to possess some other property, and because there is some truth ensuring that this stability implies the other change.

In this section I have confined myself to the second sort of case of induction, where we are concerned with possession of a property throughout a time, but it should be quite clear that the same points would apply if we discussed possession of the same property by other things of a kind. It should also be clear that although the whole discussion has proceeded using time of examination, or time of possession of a property, as the cardinal feature, the same paradox and the same solution can be unfolded without reference to time. If we take any restriction upon what has been observed in some domain – say that all objects of some class that have been observed have been observed before some time, or in some place, or by some person, or just as some conjunction of the stars took place – we can form a Goodman hypothesis differentiating others from the observed ones on the basis of their lack of possession of these properties. This is pointed out by J. J. Altham.[7] Thus if all observed emeralds have had forty-three facets, we might form the predicate "gracet":

gracet: a thing is gracet if and only if *either* the thing has forty-three facets and is green, *or* the thing has some other number of facets and is blue.

We can then imagine someone supposing that all emeralds are gracet, and someone imagining that they are all green. If it is likely that emeralds with some other number of facets will emerge at some time, which hypothesis should we accept?

Just as in the case of Goodman's own predicate, we can construct a story in which it is rational to suppose that having forty-three facets is a good ground for expecting otherwise blue gems to be green. Indeed, we are already disposed to believe that crystalline properties affect colour. But the point is that our analysis yields just as satisfactory a solution to Goodman's paradox when based on fortuitous properties of the observed phenomena as when based on time. For again we can demonstrate that the man who expects all emeralds to be gracet is expecting a *difference* between some emeralds and others. In Goodman's own case, telling grueness entails telling the time, and in this example telling that something is gracet entails telling how many facets it has, and the rest of the demonstration which I have given of the way this uncovers the bogus appearance of a similarity remains precisely the same.[8]

The general problem of projectibility which this poses is this: when, if all observed things of a sort have had two properties, is it

[7] Altham, "A Note on Goodman's Paradox", *B.J.P.S.*, 1969.

[8] The *general* epistemological criterion for differentiation is therefore this:

A predicate A differentiates things which are F from things which are not on the basis of G if (i) knowing that something is F does not entail knowing whether it is G, and (ii) knowing whether something is A does entail knowing whether it is G and whether it is F, such that if it is G and F it is A, and if it is not $\sim G$ and not $\sim F$ it is A, but not otherwise.

rational to expect a difference in one on the basis of a difference in the other? Clearly guidelines exist. If a difference in one effects a difference in the other in other similar things, or if a difference in something like one effects a difference in the other in those things, we may take this as a reason for expecting the same in our case, a reason whose strength depends upon the strength of the analogy from the other cases. Or there may be a theory with confirmation from other sources which predicts the co-variance. But in the absence of such evidence we do not differentiate, and there exists the general problem of why we are right not to do so. I shall say something about this later, but for the present we need only remember that the specific case of this which we are investigating, and to which reduce both Goodman's paradox and the classical problem of induction, is that of why we should not expect such differences solely because of the passage of time, or solely because the other things are unobserved.

Goodman and theories of induction

Goodman's problem therefore raises no difficulty for the justification of reasoning for similarities, beyond that which we started with. But although there may be nothing more to Goodman's paradox than there is to the old problem of induction, there is certainly nothing less to it. In this section I shall review briefly how certain theories of rational expectation fail to cope with the old problem if we present it in its new guise – which means that they fail to cope with the old problem, for the new guise merely reveals but does not augment its difficulty. The service rendered to epistemology by such a revelation should not be underestimated, although we must be careful of overstating the case against other theories, for even when a theory has been thought to founder on Goodman's paradox, it remains at least a possibility that our elucidation of that paradox might show that the theory actually evaded it.

Consider firstly a Bayesian confirmation theory based on some distribution of prior probabilities.[9] The essential theorem can be expressed thus:

$$\text{prob}(h, e) = \frac{\text{prob}(h) \times \text{prob}(e, h)}{\text{prob}(e)}$$

[9] Readers unfamiliar with these ideas will find an excellent introduction in Kneale, *Probability and Induction*, 1949, §§ 26, 27.

The probability of any hypothesis upon some evidence is equal to the product of the prior probability of the hypothesis, multiplied by the probability of the evidence given the hypothesis, and divided by the prior probability of the evidence. A classic problem of inductive logic is that of giving this theorem some application, the difficulty being that it's not clear when we can help ourselves to values for the antecedent probabilities. Let us then take a Goodman situation, and see how this theorem fares as a basis for preferring the non-differentiating hypothesis to the Goodman hypothesis. Suppose that we have examined a great many emeralds (under a wide variety of conditions if we like) and they have all turned out to be green; there are two hypotheses: all emeralds are green, and all emeralds are grue (in the sense of p. 63 above). Call the first hypothesis "green$_h$" and the second "grue$_h$", and the evidence "e". Then:

$$\text{prob (green}_h, e) = \frac{\text{prob (green}_h) \times \text{prob (e, green}_h)}{\text{prob (e)}}$$

$$\text{prob (grue}_h, e) = \frac{\text{prob (grue}_h) \times \text{prob (e, grue}_h)}{\text{prob (e)}}$$

What can we say to compare these values? Well, prob(e) is the same in each expression. Furthermore the probability that the evidence should be as it is, given that all emeralds are green, is identical with the probability that the evidence should be as it is, given that all emeralds are grue. For if *either* hypothesis were true, it would have been the case that any examined emerald, from however varied conditions, is green. So these two expressions cancel out, giving us:

$$(1) \qquad \frac{\text{prob (green}_h, e)}{\text{prob (grue}_h, e)} = \frac{\text{prob (green}_h)}{\text{prob (grue}_h)}$$

The ratio of the posterior probabilities, on any evidence whatsoever, is just the ratio of the prior probabilities. So in a Bayesian system, if we are ever going to find a basis for expecting a hitherto un-examined emerald to be green, we must find some way of rationally depressing the prior probabilities of Goodman hypotheses.

How can this be done? We know that the characteristic of the Goodman hypothesis is that it postulates a difference between ex-amined and unexamined emeralds, so the problem for the Bayesian

becomes one of showing that the prior probability of any such differentiating hypothesis is lower than that of a corresponding non-
differentiating hypothesis. That is, for Bayes's theorem to be any
use in discussing the problem of induction it must *first* be shown that
it is antecedently irrational to suppose that a particular difference
will occur with the same confidence as that with which we suppose
that none will occur. We have to show the antecedent irrationality
of crediting any Goodman hypothesis; Bayes's theorem cannot provide a framework in which to solve the problem of induction precisely because a solution of the problem of why not to expect
differences is a precondition of use of the theorem. Two of the three
terms which give the expression for a posterior probability fail to
discriminate between green$_h$ and grue$_h$; to show that the third does
is exactly to show that we are right not to expect differences between
the observed and the unobserved.

Faced with this point we can see how Carnap's view that equal
prior probabilities should be assigned to *structure* descriptions rather
than *state* descriptions is precisely the point which a Humean, or
Goodmanian, sceptic about induction would refuse to accept. Let us
imagine a very simple case, which demonstrates neatly how this view
of Carnap's amounts to a decision to depress the prior probability of
any hypothesis which expects a difference, and in so doing must
bear the whole weight of the anti-sceptical position. We imagine
that there are three emeralds, e_1, e_2, e_3, and two possibilities, green
and blue. There are eight state descriptions, and four structure
descriptions:

state descriptions			structure descriptions
e_1	e_2	e_3	s_1: All three green
G	G	G	s_2: Two green, one blue
G	G	B	s_3: Two blue, one green
G	B	G	s_4: All three blue
G	B	B	
B	G	G	
B	G	B	
B	B	G	
B	B	B	

Suppose that two of the emeralds have been observed, and found
to be green. Then either the state of affairs represented in the first
row of the state descriptions, or that represented in the second row,

must obtain. The second corresponds to the truth of a Goodman or differentiating hypothesis, the first to the truth of a straight hypothesis. If equal prior probabilities had been assigned to each of them, their probabilities would remain equal, i.e. the evidence would be irrelevant to expectation of greenness or blueness of the last emerald. But Carnap assigns equal prior probabilities to each of $s_1 \ldots s_4$. The result of this is clear. GGG is the only instance of s_1, and therefore has a prior probability of $\frac{1}{4}$. But GGB is one of three instances of s_2, and therefore has a prior probability of only $\frac{1}{3} \times \frac{1}{4}$. So the probability of any particular expectation of a difference, such as GGB, is depressed by this manoeuvre, which therefore affords a way of selecting prior probabilities which discriminates against those hypotheses which postulate a difference, and gives the requisite ground for a theory of evidence. The question is of course why $s_1 \ldots s_4$ should be assigned equal prior probabilities, rather than the eight state descriptions. Carnap early realised that his inductive logic was powerless against Goodman's paradox, but as we have seen this is to admit that it is powerless against the problem of induction.

Equation (1) has an interesting technical consequence, namely that the ratio of the posterior and prior probabilities of green$_h$ is identical with that of grue$_h$. This ratio might plausibly be taken as a measure of the strength of a reason; yet, whatever we say about prior probabilities, it would then emerge that our evidence is just as strong that all emeralds are grue as that they are all green. It would be just as good a reason for one as for the other. Of course it is not mandatory for a Bayesian confirmation theory to take this ratio as a measure of strength of reasons (for the wide variety of actual measures, see H. Kyburg)[10] and some actual theories (Carnap, Rescher, quoted in Kyburg) make the measure of strength of reasons proportional to the prior probabilities of the hypotheses, in which case the rationale for depressing these for the Goodman hypotheses will equally make the evidence a better reason for the non-Goodman hypothesis.

Another view of rational expectation makes elimination of alternative hypotheses, and the survival of tests, the fundamental desideratum for any hypothesis in whose predictions we can repose confidence. Let us take an eliminative theory of confirmation first. By an eliminative theory I mean one which sees the justification for a

[10] Kyburg, "Recent Work in Inductive Logic", *American Philosophical Quarterly*, 1964, p. 257.

proposition of the form 'e *R* h' in the fact that the occurrence of e eliminated (falsified) other hypotheses than h, while not of course falsifying h. The difficulty posed by Goodman's paradox is perfectly clear. Consider the continuum of hypotheses representable as 'my lawn is omnitemporally GRUE'[11] with different values of t. These all provide alternatives to the non-differentiating hypothesis that my lawn is omnitemporally green. But if at any time I look at my lawn and see that it has remained green, then although I have eliminated some GRUE hypotheses (with any present or past value of t), there remain an unlimited number of GRUE hypotheses (those with future values of t) which I have not eliminated, but alternatives to which I have eliminated. So at any time there remain an unlimited number of hypotheses which have received as much confirmation through the elimination of alternatives as the straightforward hypothesis that my lawn is omnitemporally green.

The situation appears to be the same if we describe the matter in terms of survival of strenuous tests rather than elimination of conflicting hypotheses. For naturally, any test which the 'omnitemporally green' hypothesis can now survive, any 'omnitemporally GRUE' (with future t) hypothesis can now survive: it is only later that survival of the fittest entails falsification of the less fit, and at any given later time the class of the fittest remains infinitely numerous. There are however two moves open here to a Popperian theory of confirmation.

Firstly, consider the statement: "a theory is the better confirmed the more ingenious our unsuccessful attempts at its refutation have been".[12] There is an intensionality in the notion of an attempt to refute a theory which could be of interest. Consider that where two hypotheses are each compatible with evidence which represents an unsuccessful attempt to falsify one of them, it by no means follows that the evidence represents an unsuccessful attempt to falsify the other. For the experimenter might not even have thought of the other, let alone attempted to falsify it. So imagine an attempt to falsify the hypothesis that all emeralds are green – say an attempt to dig up an emerald from a gem-bearing stratum of rock which tends to leak colourful impurities into the stones. An emerald is found, but, surprisingly, it is green. This test must have been

[11] Defined: At any time t a thing is GRUE at t if and only if either (t $<$ T & x is green) or (t $>$ T & x is blue). See Fig. 2, p. 90.

[12] Popper, *Logic of Scientific Discovery*, p. 401.

conducted at a time, say during 1970, so while the 'all emeralds are green' hypothesis survives it, so does the 'all emeralds are grue' hypothesis, with T = midnight, New Year's Eve, 1970. But while the search in such a stratum may have been an ingenious and unsuccessful attempt to falsify the hypothesis that all emeralds are green, it is exceedingly unlikely that the gemmologists, who do not on the whole read much philosophy of science, were attempting to falsify the hypothesis that all emeralds are grue. So this is *not* an ingenious and unsuccessful attempt to refute that hypothesis, and so taking strictly the statement above, no credit is due to the differentiating hypothesis on a Popperian theory.

This is an interesting move, but I am afraid it reveals a weakness in Popper's statement of his position rather than in Goodman's problem – or Hume's. For consider the following situation. I know of two hypotheses to explain a phenomenon, both of which may be false, but only one of which may be true. Another scientist is aware of the first of my theories, but not of the second, and he conducts an ingenious and powerful test for my first theory, against a third, pet theory of his own. My first hypothesis survives this test (which falsifies his pet theory perhaps) and *so does my second*. Now taking Popper's statement strictly, we could only allow my first hypothesis any credit from this experiment, for it is that alone which the rival experimenter *attempted* to falsify: he hadn't thought about my other theory. But if antecedently it was reasonable to have as much confidence in my second as in my first hypothesis, then it is quite absurd to take my first as favoured as against my second by the experimental event simply on the grounds that it was that hypothesis which the experimenter was attempting to falsify. (Of course, if the test was a more stringent test of the first than of the second, the situation would be different, but we are not supposing that.)

Again, suppose we have ingeniously attempted to falsify some hypothesis by a number of means, and failed. Suddenly someone suggests an alternative hypothesis, desirable on some ground (perhaps simplicity or derivability from an independently plausible theory) which is consistent with the results of all our experiments. It would be quite ludicrous to deny that this hypothesis is worthy of confidence because of its fit with these experimental results, which would have falsified it had they turned out otherwise, even although they were not collected as the result of attempts to falsify it, but as the result of attempts to falsify a quite different theory. In other words, the important fact about a theory and a test – and this is quite consistent with Popper's general view – is that the test should be stringent and the theory survive it, not that the test should be the result of an attempt to do one thing rather than another. But then the intensionality is removed, and we are back with the fact that when the gemmologist finds a green emerald in the strange stratum, grue$_h$ has survived the test exactly as well as green$_h$.

There is however another move open to Popperian theorists here, which raises an extremely important general point. Consider Popper's treatment of the similar problem of hypotheses of co-variation of two features given their values at different points: the problem of which line is best supported by a number of points on a graph. The problem arises because, if we consider Fig. 1, the hypothesis that the co-variation of x and y is best described by the straight line A, and that it is best described by B, are equally falsifiable intuitively: the occurrence of an indisputable reading at ϕ would falsify both.

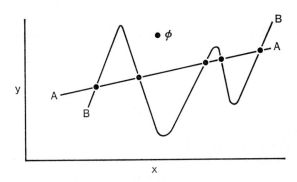

Figure 1

How then can a system taking falsifiability as its desideratum account for the feeling that A is better supported than B by the data? Popper, as is well known, answers that B is a curve of more dimensions than A, meaning that many more points have to be established to determine that the co-variation is not described by a curve like B, than have to be established to determine that it is not described by a straight line.[13] If we consider, for example, circles and straight lines, it takes only three points to falsify the straight line hypothesis, whereas it takes at least four to falsify the circle hypothesis (for a

---

[13] Popper, ch. VI.

circle can be drawn through any three points). This answer establishes a falsifiability ranking amongst *types of hypotheses*. If one scientist says "I think it's an ellipse", and the other, "I think it's a cricle" and a third "I think it's a straight line", it requires much more work (six points) to refute the first than to refute the second (four points) or the third (three points).

Let us put a differentiating hypothesis in these terms (see Fig. 2).

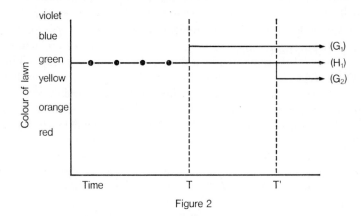

Figure 2

(H$_1$) is the hypothesis that my lawn is omnitemporally green,
(G$_1$) that it is omnitemporally GRUE (change when t $=$ T), and
(G$_2$) another Goodman hypothesis, that it is omnitemporally GREL-LOW (change when t $=$ T').

Are not these equally falsifiable? The Popperian point is that (G$_1$) and (G$_2$) are each hypotheses of a type which is less falsifiable than the straight hypothesis. What this means is: the proposition that *some Goodman hypothesis* describes the colour of the lawn is less falsifiable than the proposition that *some non-differentiating hypothesis* describes the colour of the lawn. For if we describe our belief just by saying 'some Goodman hypothesis describes the colour of the lawn', we are not refuted as long as the lawn stays green, *or* changes colour, as long as it does not change colour twice. Whereas the hypothesis that it is omnitemporally of one colour is falsified if it can be established to have changed colour once. In other words, the meta-hypothesis that some Goodman hypothesis is true is less falsifiable than the meta-hypothesis that some non-differentiating hypothesis is true, in the straightforward sense that there can be a situation where the one-colour theorist is refuted but the Goodman theorist not, but not vice versa. Another way to see this is to see that the one meta-hypothesis is:

(M) $(Ef, g)(t)(t < T \supset$ my lawn is f at t) &
$(t > T \supset$ my lawn is g at t)

where f, g are variables ranging over colours. The one-colour meta-hypothesis is logically equivalent to this *and* the constraint that $f = g$, whence its extra falsifiability. I shall call (M) with this constraint added (C). (C) is of course logically equivalent to:

(C) $(Ef)(t)$ (my lawn is f at t)

So far Popper's point is clear enough. The position is exactly the same as with the problem of co-variation, where again Popper can establish a falsifiability ranking amongst the different meta-hypotheses claiming that the true hypothesis is that the line is an ellipse, a circle, a straight line, and so on. But now we must ask what the significance of this result is. For the original problem for Popper to solve arises because (G_1) appears to be just as falsifiable as (H_1), or as (G_2): by what sleight of hand is this problem removed when we discover that (C) is more falsifiable than (M)?

The answer of course is that this problem cannot be removed. (G_1), (H_1) and (G_2) are all equally falsifiable, for each makes an equally specific prediction about the colour of the same lawn at any time. Any methodology then which makes relative falsifiability of equally corroborated hypotheses the sole criterion of choice between them gives no reason for preferring (H_1) to (G_1). But the interest of Popper's move is not its inadequacy to removing an objection to his position as it is usually stated, but its raising the question: why is (G_1)'s relation to (M) and (H_1)'s relation to (C) relevant to decision between them?

The feeling that one has is that to come to (G_1) as a preferred instance of (M) is essentially *arbitrary*. Why choose just those values of the variables – why, given that you expect the lawn to change colour, expect it to change just then to just blue? How can an argument develop between someone holding (G_1) and someone holding (G_2)? In short, the trouble with a policy of expecting differences is that there is no guidance as to which differences to expect, or when. These reactions to the Goodman hypothesis (G_1) are important, and I shall have more to say about them later. But for the present we must note that they introduce an entirely different desideratum to that of falsifiability. For the point now is that if we have, because of our past observations, an hypothesis which is a substitution instance of (C) (say, my lawn is omnitemporally green), to produce an equally falsifiable hypothesis from the less falsifiable meta-hypothesis (M) demands an apparently arbitrary assignation of value to two variables. But the avoidance of arbitrariness is not the creation of falsifiability, it is an entirely different norm. (Also, we can see the arbitrary assignation of values to variables in the creation of falsifiable hypotheses as a *daring, scientific* act of creating an *improbable* theory.) More importantly it seems doubtful whether a convinced anti-inductivist can accuse the Goodman hypothesis (G_1) of arbitrariness. For the meta-hypothesis (C) results from (M) by the restriction $f = g$. But this is just as arbitrary a restriction for the anti-inductivist. For he is producing a more falsifiable meta-hypothesis from a less falsifiable one by an arbitrary restriction on the value of one of the variables, g. Starting with (M) it seems to make little difference in point of arbitrariness, for a Popperian, whether we go via (C) to (H_1) or directly to (G_1): in either case the end product is the creation, by "arbitrary" restriction, of an equally falsifiable hypothesis.

An arbitrary assignment of values to the variables, or an arbitrary restriction on the value of one variable making it identical with the value of another, here means: one such that no reason can be given why some other assignment or restriction of values should not have been adopted. We can get equally falsifiable hypotheses from (M) by stipulating: $(f = g = $ green) or $(f = $ green, $g = $ blue, t = T) or $(f = $ green, $g = $ yellow, t = T'). Each is equally arbitrary from the Popperian standpoint, because no reason can be given in terms of falsifiability of the result for one restriction rather than another. The important general point is that once a theory of reasoning cannot separate a specific Goodman hypothesis from a straightforward one, it is no good it levelling an accusation of "arbitrariness" at the way the specificity is achieved. For if the criteria of reasoning were sufficient to show that this arbitrariness was both damaging *and* avoided by the straightforward hypothesis, then, contrary to supposition, they would directly distinguish between the Goodman and the straightforward hypothesis.

Another example of this comes with the approach which sees induction as vindicated because it is a way or the only way or the best way to achieve the aim of true prediction (Feigl, Kneale, Salmon, and many others).[14] Suppose then that you adopt (H_1) of my lawn, and I adopt (G_1). In what way are you acting in accordance with the best or the only way of making true predictions whereas I am not? What is quite certain, and what all these authors would readily admit, is that I might be right and you wrong; still, even if on isolated occasions, or not so isolated ones, I am right, nevertheless it must be held that I am predicting in a way, or in accordance with a policy, which cannot achieve the aim of truth.

The best way to see the force behind this idea is to consider (M) again. Imagine someone following the policy: "Adopt a hypothesis which gives a value to t, f, g such that $f \neq g$." This policy is that of expecting a difference. Then, whatever the course of experience, it is logically impossible that more than a minute proportion of the hypotheses which accord with this policy should be true. Because, for every one which is true there are many others which are false: for every difference which occurs, there are many other differences which don't. If a thing turns blue at a time, it does not turn green at that time, nor yellow nor orange. A change has to be a change in just one direction out of all the possible ones: it is logically necessary that most changes will not occur, so logically necessary that most of the hypotheses which could be formed and accord with the policy cited are false.

But this will not overwhelm a coherent holder of (G_1). For, he should say, the fact that his hypothesis accords with such an unimpressive policy does not matter. After all (H_1) and all the others accord with the policy of expecting the lawn always to have some colour (possibly changing) at any time, and necessarily most hypotheses according with this policy are false. An hypothesis can have extremely solid virtue in spite of according with a bad policy, and in his view (G_1) has the solid virtue that it will be shown to be true.

The point is that again we have succeeded, as Popper did, in pointing out a difference between the policy "Expect the lawn (or things in general) to change" on the one hand, and "Expect the lawn (or things in general) to stay the same" on the other. This

[14] Feigl, "De Principiis non Disputandum...?" in Black, *Philosophical Analysis*, 1950, p. 113; Kneale, *Probability and Induction*, p. 234; Salmon, "Regular Rules of Induction", *Philosophical Review*, 1956 p. 385.

time it is the difference that most predictions which could be made in accordance with the former, but not the latter, must be false. But how is this difference to be translated into differing degrees of rationality of (G_1) and (H_1)? It is quite clear that the statement of the aim of induction – true prediction – cannot achieve this translation. For again we know that (G_1) might just as well achieve this aim as (H_1): and, so long as this is so, a view which relies *solely* upon comparison in terms of achievement of true prediction, cannot use as a reason against (G_1) its 'arbitrary' selection from a class of hypotheses most of which will not provide true prediction.

The point can be put most succinctly in terms of a diagrammatic representation (Fig. 3) of the problem of induction, using the same example as that of Fig. 2.

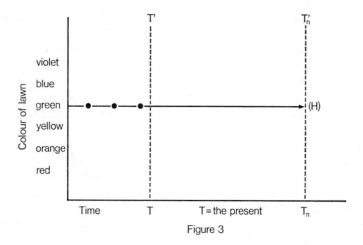

Figure 3

(H) represents the hypothesis that the lawn will stay green until T_n. If $n = \infty$ this is the hypothesis that the lawn will always be green. Now (H) represents one route among many through the continuum of points in the area $T'\,T_n'\,T_n\,T$. From Hume's point of view *any* choice of such a route is arbitrary, albeit natural to make one choice rather than another. So (H) itself suffers, according to the sceptic, just as much as any particular differentiating hypothesis, from coming from a family most of the members of which are false. For (H) is one of the (non-denumerable) infinity of routes through the area, and it is logically necessary that most of the hypotheses traced by such routes are false – (H) does not differ from a particular differentiating hypothesis G in this respect, for both come from bad families, and if we hold it against G that it is an arbitrary choice from a family of hypotheses most of which must be false, so we should hold it against (H) too. To defeat this reply it is clearly necessary to show that (H) isn't an arbitrarily chosen member of a bad family in the way that any particular alternative route would be.

In fact both Kneale and Salmon supplement their view by other principles of reasoning which might discriminate against (G_1) in favour of (H_1). For Kneale has principles of avoidance of extravagance and negligence, and Salmon reinforces his position in face of Goodman's paradox (brought against it in Barker[15]) by ad hoc principles designed to exclude Goodman hypotheses.[16] As we have seen, the exclusion of Goodman's hypotheses *is* the problem of induction, so whatever supplementary principles are needed to cope with them bear the whole weight of that problem.

This section is not an exhaustive account of theories of induction, nor an exhaustive critique of those which I mention. In it I have tried to demonstrate the way in which a correct apprehension of Goodman's problem clarifies the inadequacy of certain theories of rational expectation. But there may easily be theories which are not shown to be hollow by its means. In particular I have not discussed the possibility that the simplicity of expecting a resemblance rather than a difference may be important. But the demand we make of reasoning is reliability, not simplicity, so this popular point will not tempt us from the honest toil of finding some connection between expecting a resemblance, and being right.

Conclusion

In this chapter we have seen how Goodman's paradox reduces to the old problem of why to expect the unobserved to be like the observed, and that the principal interest of the paradox[17] is that, in

---

[15] Barker, "Comments on Salmon's Vindication of Induction", in Feigl and Maxwell, *Current Issues in the Philosophy of Science*, 1961, p. 257.

[16] Salmon, "On Vindicating Induction", in Kyburg and Nagel, *Induction: Some Current Issues*, 1963.

[17] Apart, perhaps, from the interest of the issues in philosophical logic which are raised in the reduction of the paradox to the old problem.

putting the old problem as one of choice between resemblances and differences, it provides a good way of assessing the adequacy of proposed answers to the old problem. In particular we saw the way in which the use of Bayesian confirmation theory must presuppose the solution of the old problem, and the way in which falsification and vindication approaches fail. The trap is that although they can each make general points about someone who says "I expect a difference" as opposed to someone who says "I expect a resemblance", they are powerless to criticise somebody who announces that he expects some particular difference.

One of the results of the second half of this work is that we can give force to the charge that such an expectation is arbitrary. We can derive from this that it is unreasonable to trust it. But for this derivation a version of a principle of indifference is needed – a principle which tells us that if most expectations of a certain sort are false, and that nothing more is known about a particular expectation than that it is of that sort, then it is unreasonable to trust it. Of course this still will not amount to a defence of an expectation of a resemblance: reference to Fig. 3 reminds us that so far it is in the same boat. So I now turn to the task of defending principles of reasoning which separate a resemblance from a difference and which entitle us to confidence in the one but not the other. These principles will not, however, seem very attractive if the discussion is presented in terms of probabilities. This is a notion which I have deliberately avoided until now. But for the second half of the work to achieve anything convincing we must see how it relates to the usual demand that conclusions of inductive reasoning must be shown to be probable.

5
Probability and reasons

Introduction

At the end of chapter 2 we had established a connection between using a reason, and using something which generally furthers the aim of having confidence in the truth. At the end of the last chapter we saw that any useful analysis must be able to pin a damaging charge of arbitrariness on a particular case of expecting a change. We must be able to put to effect the point that although a particular differentiating hypothesis might on occasion be true, such things must, logically, be generally false. So what we need is an elucidation of the principles which entitle us to believe that a particular thing has a feature when we know that things of its sort generally have that feature. At this point it is tempting to protest that this theory is already extant: it is the theory of probability. And many philosophers might hold that the detailed discussion of the concept of a reason and of the connection between reasoning and truth could have been avoided had we availed ourselves of this prominent notion.

Of course it is not as though the theory of probability has been given a generally acceptable application to the problem of induction. Indeed we saw in the final section of the last chapter that a great deal of the formal elaboration of the theory commonly found in works on induction is not going to advance the problem of justification, for, insofar as it has to justify assigning lower prior probability to differentiating hypotheses, any theory based on Bayes's theorem has to sink the problem before it can bring its apparatus to bear upon it. Shortly I shall be advancing certain principles of reasoning which provide a key to the problem of justification, but these will appear problematic if they are framed using the concept of probability. I want now to prepare the ground for the view that this doesn't matter. It should always be remembered that the two notions which we must link are I-evidence on the one hand and the increase of confidence in an I-prediction on the other. If we allow an intermediary such as the probability of a change, or the probability of a prediction, to occupy the foreground of our thoughts, we simply run the risk that its own opacity screens things which would other-wise be clear. I shall argue that this is almost inevitable since the concept of probability contains features whose mutual reconciliation is almost impossible. If the application of the concept of probability is as haphazard as I claim, then it is no wonder that argument can be brought against any attempt to prove that I-predictions are really probable when suitable I-evidence exists. But it may be really reason-able to repose confidence in them for all that. In this chapter I shall try to substantiate the charge that the internal stresses in the concept of probability are too great for it to be anything other than a hind-rance in our problem.

Subjective aspects of the concept

From the very beginning philosophers discussing the concept of probability have been torn between two apparently conflicting aspects of the notion, which can be labelled its subjective and objec-tive facets. As Keynes puts it:

> "It is agreed that there is a sort of probability which depends upon knowledge and ignorance, and is relative, in some manner, to the mind of the subject; but it is supposed that there is also a more objective Probability which is not thus dependent, or less completely so, though precisely what this conception stands for is not plain."[1]

But there is no easy way of showing that the word and its cognates are ambiguous: what we have is a difficulty in the understanding of one concept, rather than a straightforwardly ambiguous word. Why then do so many writers feel the opposing pulls when they come to treat the notion?

Put in terms of probability the thing that interests us about I-predictions is the probability or improbability of a regularity con-tinuing. And this is the same as the improbability or probability of a corresponding *event*, namely a change. So to bring out the interest-ing features of the notion I shall use an example in which the subject is the probability of an event:

(Pr) The probability of Eclipse winning the 2.30 is very high.

[1] Keynes, *Treatise on Probability*, p. 281. The following pages give interesting historical references.

I shall start by selecting argument about (Pr) as an indicative feature of its meaning. The first thing that strikes us is that there is no obvious difference between argument about (Pr) and argument about whether Eclipse will win the 2.30.[2] I would use precisely the same facts to try to convince you that the probability of Eclipse winning is high that I would use to try to convince you that Eclipse will win. It is not as though I could come up to an argument about the 2.30 with a piece of information about Eclipse, and before knowing whether my information is relevant to the argument have to wait to discover if the argument concerned whether Eclipse would win, or whether the probability was high that he would win. It is not as though a judge of a debate could rule that disputant A has the best case for saying that the probability of Eclipse winning is high, but disputant B the best case for saying that Eclipse will win. To all intents and purposes, argument about the probability of an event is argument about whether it will occur. This significant fact is most cautiously summed up in the following Argument Condition:

(AC) No fact which can be brought to an argument is relevant if the argument concerns the probability of an event, but irrelevant if it concerns whether the event will occur, or vice versa.

What then if an argument convinces us, and we assent to (Pr)? Again we have the connection with supposing that Eclipse will win, with a degree of confidence commensurate with the value we give the probability. Consider for example *acting as though* we assent to (Pr). Suppose that a gangster tells his man to go and act as though he accepted that the probability of Eclipse winning is very high. What does his man do? He frequents racing circles, is seen betting on Eclipse, praises the horse, laughs at the competition, emphasises his good points. In fact in everything he acts as though he wanted it to be known that *he has great confidence that Eclipse will win*. And it is not through lack of acting ability that this is all that he can do; it is not as though there is a nuance of assent to (Pr) which a gangster is unlikely to catch; all that he can do or was expected to do is to betray high confidence in Eclipse winning. Again, imagine a tipster telling me (Pr), and next being observed

[2] Unobvious differences might arise if we were arguing about the sort of case analysed on p. 37.

busily acting as though Eclipse would not win: specifically, taking his money off Eclipse. There is, it seems, no alternative but either to call him insincere or accept that he changed his mind. Altogether then, we can sum up assent to (Pr) in a Consequence Condition:

> (CC) Assent to the supposition that the probability of an event is very high has the same consequences for action as assent with a high degree of confidence (but not complete assurance) to the supposition that the event will occur.

Of course, this does not mean that if you assent to (Pr) you ought immediately to bet on Eclipse: you can accept (Pr) and refuse to do anything about it, or want to "wait and see", just as some time before a race you can believe that Eclipse will win, and not do anything about it, or want to "wait and see".

The two conditions (AC) and (CC) suggest very strongly an illocutionary theory of probability, whereby saying that the probability of an event is high is construed as a way of saying that the event will occur, and as saying nothing different to that. To my knowledge, the only writer to follow this suggestion is Toulmin, who thinks that a sentence such as (Pr) is used to make a guarded assertion that Eclipse will win, and that, in general, the use of "it is probable that", "it is likely that", "probably", "the probability of. . .is high", is to indicate just the speaker's degree of hesitation about the event considered.[3]

This is an attractive view: because it accounts so nicely for (AC) and (CC); because it provides such a simple analysis of the concept, leaving mathematical elaboration of evidence from frequencies to statistics rather than including them in the analysis of an everyday notion; becuse it preserves the view that probability is the guide of life, inasmuch as our confidence in various things, in varying degrees, is certainly the guide of life. Furthermore one step will connect this view with the views of "subjectivists" about probability like Ramsey and de Finetti.[4] If we suppose that a speaker's degree

---

[3] Toulmin, "Probability", in *Essays in Conceptual Analysis*, ed. Flew, 1963, pp. 157–91. Lucas, *The Concept of Probability*, 1970, p. 2, approves, but also thinks that to ascribe a high probability to a proposition is to make an objective claim, and, absurdly, one inconsistent with the claim that the proposition is true (p. 21 and *passim*).

[4] F. P. Ramsey, "Truth and Probability", *The Foundations of Mathematics*, 1931; de Finetti, "Foresight: Its Logical Laws, its Subjective

of hesitation is adequately represented by how he would bet in a certain type of situation, then numerically precise statements of probability can be regarded in exactly the same way. In making them a speaker is expressing that degree of hesitation shown by somebody prepared to bet at a corresponding rate in a certain situation. Since it is necessarily irrational to bet so that whatever the outcome one loses, the ordinary axioms of probability can be deduced as constraints upon rational betting. Indeed these are quite properly taken as constraints on rational degrees of confidence, for exactly the subjectivists' reasons.

It should be clear that if this were the whole truth about probability the introduction of the notion could neither help nor hinder our investigation. For a demand to show that the probability of a prediction is high would be just the demand to show that the prediction is true, although a demand framed and therefore satisfied with the recognition that the answer may allow a certain amount of hesitation. We would, in sum, just have to show that I-evidence makes it right to have a high degree of confidence in an appropriately related I-proposition, but this is the way we have put the problem to ourselves all along. So if this were the whole truth about the notion it would at least be innocuous, although we would also be justified in framing the problem without reference to it. Unfortunately the matter is not so simple as that.

Objective aspects of the concept

If the subjective or illocutionary theory that (AC) and (CC) suggest is true, a proposition such as (Pr) has just the same truth conditions as 'Eclipse will win the 2.30.' But there are occasions on which we contrast and compare the truth of a probability assessment with the truth of a prediction. We can say, for example: "Of course the probability of winning is tiny, still, you never know your luck", which seems to contrast something whose truth is known with something else whose truth is not; or: "I don't know whether it will happen, and I don't even know how probable it is", which seems to involve the view that there are two different things to be ignorant of. We can even deliberately contrast a belief about the probability

Sources", translation in *Studies in Subjective Probability*, ed. Kyburg and Smokler, 1964.

with out own attitude to the prediction, as in: "Zenith has entered, so I'm afraid the probability of Eclipse winning alters a bit, but I'm going to leave my money where it is. It's a funny thing but I still feel confident about the result." The impression that these examples give, that we sometimes treat probability as a quantity whose value entails nothing about the occurrence of the event, is reinforced, fatally for Toulmin's theory, if we consider tensed probability ascriptions.

Consider:

(Pr2) The probability of Eclipse winning was high.
(Pr2$_p$) The probability of Eclipse winning was high but he didn't.
(Pr3) The probability that Eclipse won is high.

Statements such as (Pr2$_p$) are widely thought to provide a difficulty for Toulmin's view, and indeed Toulmin himself devotes a considerable amount of space to their discussion. But the feature which is supposed to be uncomfortable is the contrast between the event *being* probable and it not *happening*. Toulmin, discussing the "improbable" stories of Marco Polo, says:

> ". . .we therefore have no business to describe them as ever having 'been improbable', since for us to do this tends in some measure to lend our authority to a view which we know to be false." (p. 168)

It seems that the view to which we would wrongly lend our authority is that the stories weren't true: Toulmin's theory seems to be that to say that something was improbable is to say that it didn't happen, and to say it guardedly, in which case (Pr2$_p$) would be a contradiction of which one conjunct is asserted guardedly.

But the real difficulty lies not with (Pr2$_p$), but with the difference between (Pr2) and (Pr3). On Toulmin's illocutionary theory, to assert (Pr3) is to assert guardedly that Eclipse won. It would naturally be said when the race had happened and we hadn't heard the results. But what then of (Pr2)? The discussion of Marco Polo above shows that Toulmin thinks that (Pr2) too makes a guarded assertion that Eclipse won (which is why it is not to be coupled with an unguarded one that he didn't). But that identifies (Pr2) and (Pr3), for each is said to make guardedly the assertion that Eclipse won. But if one thing is certain, it is that (Pr2) and (Pr3) are not identical.

Nor is this a slip on Toulmin's part. It is a quite central difficulty of the illocutionary theory. For you can tense a verb, and tense an assertion, but you cannot tense a way of making an assertion. But it is just this that we can do with probability: a probability may be high, may have been high, and perhaps will be high. So it is not, as Toulmin and his critics think, that his theory gives a certain account of (Pr2) which is open to discussion; it is rather that it gives no account of (Pr2) at all, and the supposition that it does arises from the confusion of (Pr2) with the quite different (Pr3).

We can sum all this up as a Tense Condition:

(TC) We can say that the probability of an event was high at some time previous to its occurrence or failure to occur, and this is not to say that it is now probable that it did happen.

For the present I shall postpone discussion of whether the probability of an event can have been high, and the event not have happened.

The tense condition gives a very strong impression that a past tense probability assertion describes some past state of affairs, and that confidence that this state existed is logically independent of confidence that the event said to be probable happened. More evidence that a probability sentence expresses a proposition with different truth conditions from a straightforward prediction of an event arises if we consider changing probabilities. We might say: "The probability of Eclipse winning has gone down drastically", and we all know when this would be agreed upon. The entry of strong competition, the contraction of some ailment, rain when he likes hard going, or in general the deterioration of some condition affecting the outcome of the race, would lower the probability of his victory. Furthermore it appears that something which affects or might affect the outcome of the race must alter if the probability of Eclipse winning is to alter. If we imagine our gangster ordering his man to decrease the probability of Eclipse winning, the only way in which he can be obeyed is for his man to tamper in some way with the set-up, by doping Eclipse, entering a stronger horse, etc. This logical requirement on changing probability can be expressed in a Supervenience Condition:

(SC) A change in the probability of an event entails a change in some of the conditions which affect or may be going to affect the occurrence of the event.

It is extremely important to notice that (SC) is a logical requirement on the probability of an *event*. Its analogue for the probability of a proposition or hypothesis is not true. For we normally think that the acquisition of certain evidence will change the probability of a proposition. But that somebody collects more evidence is not normally one of the things which affects or may be going to affect the truth of the prediction. When we find that Eclipse has 'flu we *discover* that the probability of his winning is very low, we don't *make* the probability of his winning very low. It is his catching 'flu which ruins his chances, not our discovery of it. This means of course that one familiar type of analysis is certainly going to be inadequate to propositions like (Pr). If we attempt an analysis which sees (Pr) as asserting a relationship between the prediction that Eclipse will win and, say, our total available evidence, it will simply misrepresent what would change the probability of Eclipse winning. For consider what would change the truth of: 'The proposition that event e will occur is well supported by the total available evidence.' Clearly, the discovery of evidence pointing the other way. But that just corrects our estimate of Eclipse's chances, it doesn't alter his chances. The gangster's assistant does not obey his command to change the probability of Eclipse winning ("Dish Eclipse's chances") by diligently searching for evidence, even if he changes the truth of 'the proposition that Eclipse will win is well supported by the total available evidence' thereby. Such an analysis then gives a proposition whose truth depends upon entirely different conditions to those upon which the analysandum depends, and is therefore incorrect.

So far then we have some reason to regard statements attributing probability to an event at a time as making real assertions about some state of the world at that time. But what then could the truth conditions of such assertions be? I think we can prove that there is no hope of identifying empirical conditions which give a guarantee of a probability assessment, in the following way.

Let us imagine arguing with someone extremely knowledgeable about what the world is like now, and about what natural laws exist. (Under his knowledge of what the world is like now I mean to include knowledge of what dispositional properties, like brittleness or biasedness, objects possess.) This man knows a great many, perhaps all, propositions whose truth conditions exist now, and knows too all natural laws. So he is extremely well placed in any argument about what will happen, for although I haven't invested

him directly with knowledge of the future, I have given him knowledge from which he can infer a great deal about the future. Call
this man the Present Tense Knowledgeable Being: PKB for short.
Now I say to the PKB that the probability of Eclipse winning the
2.30 is very high. Let us suppose that he disagrees. Inevitably he
wins the argument, for he knows what Eclipse's health is like, what
his opponents' health is like, whether anyone at present intends to
dope him, what his jockey's emotional problems are, and many other
things, and he knows any laws that may exist connecting these
facts with what will occur on the day of the race. His knowledge
may indeed enable him to deduce who will win the race. Now I
start off making my probability assertion, and for each piece of
evidence I produce, the PKB can produce more, qualify my evidence,
show its lack of significance, show that other events are in train
which mean that it is irrelevant, or in some way demonstrate that
he has a better basis for prediction than me. And at each stage of the
argument I will express my defeat by admitting that *the probability
is not as high as I thought.*

Now suppose that the PKB's knowledge falls short of actually
entailing that Eclipse will or will not win. Suppose that all that he
can do is assert that the probability is that Eclipse will not win. Then
it is logically possible that there should exist a superior PKB – one
with a shade more knowledge – who could in turn use his acquaintance with what is the case to make the original PKB admit that the
probability of Eclipse winning is higher, or lower, than he took it to
be. And so we can imagine an endless hierarchy of possible revision, until eventually someone's knowledge enables him to deduce
the outcome of the race. We can express this as a Revision Condition:

(RC) For any aggregate of knowledge K about what is the case
and what laws exist, if on the basis of K we think that the
probability of an event has some value, other than 0 or 1, it
is always logically possible that someone, by adding to K,
should make us admit that the probability of the event has
some higher or lower value than we took it to have.

Of course, (SC) forbids us to suppose that the existence of a PKB
alters the probability of the event: the mere existence of a very
wise investigator is not one of the conditions normally affecting the
occurrence of events.

At this stage it might seem that our conditions (RC) and (SC) upon argument about probability lead hopelessly to the conclusion that probabilities are really all o or 1, or near to o or 1, but that in the absence of a PKB we do not know which. For if a PKB does not alter the probability of an event, and if he can always make us revise our estimate unless that reaches something near o or 1, surely it follows that the actual probability is something near o or 1, but that normally we do not know which. It seems to me that this is a desperate problem in our ordinary conception of the probability of an event. All that I have used in bringing out the problem is the aspect of the notion which leads us to regard a probability as something to be known about or ignorant of, something of which estimates can be made and progressively rectified by more and more knowledge of circumstances. And I do not see how it could be denied that there is this element in our use of the concept.

For the present we can notice that the probability of an event conceived of as a quantity of which we are always ignorant in advance, but of which progressively better estimates can be made, is of no use to the problem of induction. It introduces another proposition, apparently different from the I-proposition, about which we are ignorant, namely the proposition that an event such as a change which would refute the I-proposition has a high or low probability. But our ignorance of the probability, so conceived, has nothing to do with the rationality of belief in the I-proposition. We may be ignorant of the probability for a variety of reasons which a PKB could clear up, yet still some expectation of what will happen may be a good deal more rational than another. We have no assurance that belief that an event will occur is only rational if it is known that the probability is high, and the elements I have stressed which make this knowledge appear so problematical only serve to make it a very implausible condition upon rational belief. But we shall return to this point after a consideration of whether anything can be said to reconcile the features of probability which we have uncovered.

A possible theory

If we thought of an ascription of probability to an event as an ordinary sort of proposition whose truth consisted in the existence of a corresponding state of affairs, that state of affairs would be subject to very peculiar conditions. It is tied to ordinary empirical facts about conditions affecting the occurrence of the event by the constraint that the probability cannot change without one of these changing, as (SC) describes. But it is loose from these conditions because no particular totality of such conditions (including facts about laws and dispositions) will guarantee that the event has a given probability, since the estimate can always be revised as additions are made to the totality, unless we arrive at a guarantee that the event will or will not occur. This is what (RC) describes. The task of describing a state of affairs with this logic seems to me to be most unenviable.[5]

An alternative would be to regard "The probability of Eclipse winning the 2.30 is very high" as a sentence used to make a conversational move which is successful or not in some different way, not because of a correspondence or lack of it with some state of affairs. We have already blocked out the rough nature of the move in (AC) and (CC), but a fuller description needs to take in (SC), (RC) and (TC). Notably, the last three conditions are inapplicable to the less formal "*Probably*, Eclipse will win the 2.30." This operator cannot be tensed, and the sentences it gives rise to do not appear to express propositions in other ways. They cannot be hypothesised, for example. Toulmin's theory is therefore perfectly adequate to it, but although this should encourage us, it still shows no way of extending the insight to cover the more formal operator.

Toulmin's theory gave no account of:

(Pr4) If the probability of Eclipse winning was high, then Eclipse won

because it came to grief over the tense condition, (TC). But (Pr4) is surely false. Even if my Premium Bond won, I may quite properly describe this as an immensely improbable event, an event which didn't just seem, but really was, improbable. The significant thing is: we would say that it is true that this was an improbable event, say ten minutes before Ernie, the selection machine, was set in motion, *even* although we realise that a PKB could have had knowledge at that time which, had he produced it, would have made us agree that it was a probable event, and *even* although his presence and the production of his knowledge didn't alter the probability of my winning.

The idea that this suggests is that an assessment of a probability

[5] An identical point arises with moral discourse, and I develop the argument in "Moral Realism", in *Morality and Moral Reasoning*, ed. J. Casey, 1971.

statement as true is "conversation-relative": we are right to hold that the event was improbable, but we would have been wrong to hold that the event was improbable faced with a PKB, and wrong in any event to hold that the presence of the PKB changes the probability. The difference is that the presence of the PKB provides a different conversational milieu, differing particularly in that in it we are faced with someone who can point to *specific* facts in virtue of which our confidence in the event's occurrence is ill-founded. A claim about probability at a time will, it seems, be true and accepted as true unless someone to whom the claim is addressed has a particular piece of information about the state of things at that time which enables him to refute it. This at any rate seems roughly so. The model that it suggests is that of a conversational move with the following characteristics:

(a) Acceptance of the move normally entails possession of some confidence that the event said to be probable will occur. (CC)

(b) The move answers to the production of facts in the following way:

    (i) The move can be tensed (the probability *is*, or *was*, such and such) in which case the relevant facts concern the conditions surrounding the event *at the time* to which the move was tensed. (TC)

    (ii) The relevant facts are those which provide a reason for or against expecting the event to happen.

    (iii) The move is to be accepted, and this acceptance expressed by saying that it is true that the event has the probability described unless *either* the move is not backed by an appropriate relevant fact, *or* a further specific relevant fact appropriate to a different confidence in the event's occurrence can be produced. (AC)

(c) Acceptance of a probability statement as true is then in principle subject to revision as other, specific facts as in (b iii) are produced. (RC)

(d) On the other hand, if the facts backing a probability statement change over time, it follows that (b iii) may be satisfied for one probability assessment tensed to one time, and a different one tensed to another time. So then, and only then, can it be true to say that the probability changed. (SC)

(e) In the case of a probability assessment tensed to the past, acceptance may be dictated under (b iii), whilst it is also known whether the event happened or not. In this case we can truly say that an improbable event happened, or a probable event did not happen. In this case (a) is waived.

The reason why a move satisfying (b) should have the consequence (a) is just that what we must go on in deciding whether an event will occur is those facts we can now produce relevant to confidence in its occurrence.

This is a sketch of a theory, whose principal interest lies in the features which it attempts to take into account. By concentrating upon one feature at the expense of others we can see how other theories derive their plausibility – a subjectivist and Toulmin emphasising (CC); a relational theory emphasising (b iii); the idea that probabilities reflect ignorance (God does not use the notion) arising from (RC).

Is this model adequate? To a surprising extent I think that it is, although as I suggested at the beginning of the discussion it may be that our application of the concept is so haphazard that any attempt to rationalise it involves an element of legislation. One necessary refinement is this. It may be that on an occasion of argument about the occurrence of an event no move (saying "The probability is high" or "The probability is low") is successful, because none can be backed up by appropriate evidence in our possession. None of the participants knows enough to establish such a claim. But the participants may be reluctant to believe that no such claim is true, as they should do according to our analysis. According to our analysis the truth of the claim is a matter of the success of the move, so if the move is not successful the claim is not true. But that is not quite how we regard it. Consider for example the excellent case of the coin which is biased, but whose direction of bias is unknown. Let us suppose that our gangster turns his attention to cricket, and invents a machine for giving coins a bias, although the physical distortion is undetectable by normal means. Furthermore the machine biases one way or the other at random, so that the only way in which to tell whether a coin is biased to fall heads or tails is by tossing it a number of times. Now when a coin emerges from a machine, neither the move "The probability of heads first toss is higher than that of tails" nor the move "The probability of tails first toss is higher than that of heads" could be successful, for all the relevant evidence is entirely symmetrical. Yet everyone would regard one of them as true. Everyone would admit to being ignorant of the probability, which is regarded as an unknown quantity in spite of the failure of any claim about it. The problem for my analysis is to account for the temptation to think that one claim is true although neither is successful in terms of (b).

It is quite clear that in this situation we have a decisive but as yet unobtained piece of evidence about the coin in mind, namely, what happens when it is tossed a number of times. We know that this evidence, when it comes, will establish one claim against the other. It seemes to me that when we have such a specific piece of as yet unobtained evidence in mind, we feel entitled to enlarge the notion of truth to apply to whichever move would be successful were this obtained. We will call ourselves ignorant of the probability precisely when we are envisaging the use of such a piece of evidence which is not as yet in play. Similarly for example we might say: "Nobody can estimate the chances of there being a nuclear war next year", for although reasons can be given for supposing that there will not be one, we can think of things which might be going on and which we would really like to know about before committing ourselves – is Russia thinking of annexing Berlin, does Nixon need to placate the Pentagon, and so forth. On the other hand, with equal propriety we might maintain that we *can* estimate the chances of there being a nuclear war next year, because we can use a lot of very good evidence which will give a weight of reason on one side. It seems to me that neither claim is unquestionably the one to make. We are out of the realm of correspondence with the facts here, and after that which claim it is more appropriate to make could clearly depend upon a variety of factors. The use of a notion which allows this fluidity when we envisage further information is explained by degrees of reticence. When we recognise that our evidence is incomplete in some way we may not wish to take the responsibility of guiding someone (via (AC)) by making a successful move and asserting a probability. This fluidity of reticence, combined with the objective appearance of the assertion: "The probability of the event occurring is high", is a clear recipe for unreal dispute about the application of the concept: "Do we know the probability when. . .?" Other disadvantages emerge in the next section.

The idea of a conversationally relative move is one that it is hard to make precise. The idea is that of a number of participants (or one man conducting a monologue) pooling and then weighing their total information relevant to expecting the event. Or, if they are talking about whether a past event was probable at some time t, before it happened or failed to happen, they pool their total information about the state of the world at t, which would have been relevant to expecting the event had the discussion taken place at t. This, notice, is logically independent of whether at t it would have been reasonable to expect the event. For they may now possess information about the state of the world at t which it would have been unreasonable to expect anyone at t to possess. Nobody would therefore have been unreasonable in making a different calculation at t. If the evidence is of sufficient weight, and if no specific and important piece of evidence is agreed to be lacking, as in the coin case, they can express themselves as knowing the probability of the event.

In a different conversation, with participants who have different information, everybody may decide that he too knows the probability of the event, although he gives it a different value. What I mean by calling the move conversationally relative is that on the occasion each of the claims may have been perfectly proper, right, and indeed true in the only sense which has application. This is not to say that anybody could ever be in a position to say that two different probability claims are each true. For anybody estimating the truth of the claims has simply to conduct his own investigation of the probability of the event, and find whether either of the conflicting estimates agrees with his. If one does he can at the most call that one true. Perhaps these things seem less perplexing if we remember the nature of accepting a probability claim, namely the distribution of confidence (or a claim about the distribution of confidence to make on the basis of the state of the world at a time, if the claim is tensed to a time), and reflect that it might be right to repose confidence in a guide which is safeguarded as well as we can envisage even although in the abstract we realise that different and better techniques might exist which would guide us in a different direction. Only in some such way as this can the proper claims to knowledge of the probability be reconciled with the indefinite revisability of any estimate.

Disadvantages of using the concept

The features of the concept which I have laboured to reconcile are more important to this work than the theory I have been led to sketch. The features I have isolated are not illusory, they immediately lead to difficulties in its application, and if these difficulties are not to be resolved in the way I have suggested, then the concept is an even worse instrument to use in an analytical enterprise than I take it to be. Of course a rectified concept could be defined. It will then give rise to a rectified problem: show that certain events are or are not probable in this new rectified sense. But we have got a perfectly good problem as it is, without needing to invent notions to express new ones with.

If my theory about the concept is roughly correct, it is quite evident that putting the problem in terms of: "Show that certain I-propositions are really very probable", or: "Show that the probability of certain states continuing is really very high", in no way supersedes the problem described in terms of reasons. For to succeed in showing these things would entail showing that certain of the facts we know, by observation or memory, provide reasons for I-propositions, or for the continuation of some regularities. For until we did that, we couldn't be sure that the backing from past experience which we are inclined to give for our I-predictions, really provides a relevant fact as demanded in (b), and therefore couldn't be sure that "the probability of my carpet staying the same colour for ten minutes is very high" really is a successful move, i.e. true.

Even if my theory is substantially incorrect, the complications in the logic of the concept of probability leave the problem of justification best stated without reference to it. Firstly there is one sort of scepticism about probabilities which has no bearing on the question of what we are justified in placing confidence in. This arises with the thought that perhaps some state of affairs obtains, about which we know nothing, and which will bring about the non-fulfilment of our expectations. To use two examples of Russell's: perhaps the Universe is in the hands of a giant puppeteer who is even now preparing to drop the strings; perhaps the man who feeds the chicken is coming to wring its neck.[6] We then think: after the ensuing

---

[6] Russell, *Problems of Philosophy*, ch. 6.

catastrophe anyone would be right to say, once he discovered the antecedents of it, that the probability of the catastrophe was high all the time, although we knew nothing of it. In the same way we know, after all, that the probability of the chicken living a long life is very small. So, we think, perhaps the probability of catastrophe really is high, the probability of the world continuing in accordance with our expectations very low.

On my theory, this is not a good route to scepticism even about probabilities. For although the subsequent investigator would be right to say that the probability of catastrophe was high all the time, he has the ability to produce the relevant fact – the intentions of the puppeteer or chicken farmer – while we have not. This ensures the success of his move, the truth of his assertion. But this has a consequence not that he knows the probability, while we do not, but rather that we cannot compare unfavourably the assertions that we would make in a discussion of the probability of our expectations being borne out with the assertions that he could make. Be that as it may, it is certain that the argument has some attraction as an argument for scepticism about probability. (For even on my theory, it leads us to think that perhaps in the future someone could say truly that the probability of catastrophe was high all the time, which is a strong enough sceptical thought.) But it has no relevance at all when we consider *justifying* the expectation that a catastrophe will or will not occur. All it can indicate is that a catastrophe might occur, and the events contributing to it might already have been set in train. But of course it doesn't show that we would be right to have any confidence that this is so; indeed, precisely those things which justify us in supposing that such an expectation-nullifying catastrophe as that which befell the chicken will not occur, also justify us in supposing that no train of events is now in motion which will bring about its occurrence. In short, indicating the possibility that the world may fail to conform to our inductively based expectations may be a good way to introduce the problem, but it does not affect the problem of the justification of those expectations in a way in which it might affect, and certainly does confuse, the problem of showing that the events and states of affairs we expect really have a high probability of coming to pass. In an ordinary context the demand "Show that the probability of event e is high" and the demand "Show that it is reasonable to expect event e" each lead to the same investigation. But for the reasons I have drawn out the philosopher who questions whether we have *really* shown that the probability is high will raise more puzzlement and sympathy than one who questions whether we have *really* shown that it is reasonable to expect the event.

The second important gain which results from aiming at showing our predictions to be reasonable, rather than events to be probable, is that the way in which "the probability of the event is high" sounds to describe a fact about the world can prompt a very flat rejection of perfectly proper approaches to the matter. Thus, for example, if we admit that we are in a state of partial ignorance, and yet try to show that we *know* the probability of a prediction, it may be tempting for some philosophers to throw a blanket charge of "probability magic" or creating knowledge out of ignorance, which sounds a bad thing to try to do. But this reflex is of no avail when we aim at rationality, for the problem precisely is to put conditions upon what can be reasonably believed when we are partially ignorant.

This opens the way to a fresh look at our problem of relating a truth about how things generally are or what a policy generally achieves, to a particular case. For we might be able to make the connection using some analogue for reasons of the much despised principle of indifference for probabilities. The same moral can be drawn immediately from the case of the biased coin. For there we are in a situation of ignorance, not knowing which way the coin is biased, nor which outcome will occur more frequently in a long run of tosses of the coin. And we agree with classical writers who attack the principle of indifference in saying that in this case we do not know what the probability of heads or of tails is. But just as this admission complicates the theory I presented, so it complicates the relationship between probability and justified confidence. For perhaps in this case *equal* confidence in heads and tails is the only justified distribution of confidence, although the probability of each event is known to be other than $\frac{1}{2}$. But if we have a distinction between the situation where *it is truly believed that two alternatives are equally probable* and the situation where it is *right to have the same degree of confidence* that either event will occur, then we can raise again the question of the principle of indifference. For some arguments used against the principle – such as that, knowing nothing, we could use it to infer that heads and tails are equally probable even when the coin is biased – become irrelevant. For knowing nothing, or even knowing that the coin is biased, it may be right to have equal confidence in heads and tails. So, ignoring probability, the question remains of whether we could use some form of the principle to put conditions on how we should distribute our confidence when ignorant, and thereby provide a foundation for justifying some of our expectations. It is to this question that we now turn.

6

The principle of indifference

Kneale's view

We are now searching for a principle, or principles, which will enable us to connect the fact that something is generally the case with the rationality of a particular belief. We are considered to be in a situation of partial ignorance, and our ignorance embraces metaphysical theses, such as the thesis that a limited number of types of change are possible, which have been supposed necessary to give objective probabilities to our predictions. I conjectured that this freedom raises again the possibility of giving some application to the notorious "principle of indifference". Since few philosophical principles are more universally eschewed, I shall start by using one of the best attacks upon it as an aid to giving a proper formulation of the ideas involved.

Kneale characterises the mistake which classical writers on probability made in using the principle of indifference as that of using "absence of knowledge" instead of "knowledge of absence" as a "sufficient ground for judgments of probability".[1] He says:

> "I have argued that we are entitled to treat alternatives as equiprobable if, but only if, we know that the available evidence does not provide a reason for preferring any one to any other. According to the principle of indifference we may call alternatives equiprobable if we do not know that the available evidence provides a reason for preferring any one to any other. Instead of knowledge of absence Laplace and those who agree with him accept absence of knowledge as a sufficient ground for judgments of probability."

He continues:

> "According to the principle of indifference alternatives are equiprobable if I am indifferent in my attitudes towards them. According to the theory I have put forward it is necessary that

[1] Kneale, *Probability and Induction*, p. 173.

the alternatives themselves should be indifferent, i.e. without difference in a certain respect."[2]

Now I think it is not at all clear from this passage just what mistake the writers who agree with Laplace made. The first difficulty is that Kneale's two descriptions of what follows according to the principle of indifference are rather different, although neither of them is completely straightforward. The first passage gives sufficient conditions for the situation where, according to the respect theories, we are "entitled to treat" alternatives as equiprobable, or "may call" them equiprobable. Now I think these phrases must mean the same here, for otherwise we do not get a straight contrast between the two theories, in terms of what, according to each of them, we may call, or are entitled to treat as, equiprobable. But what do they both mean? In particular, are we being told what, according to these theories, we may *truly* call equiprobable, or what we may *reasonably* or without irrationality call equiprobable?

The second passage describes the differences in terms of what the theories actually take to *be* equiprobable, and hence presumably of what we may *truly* call equiprobable, according to them. So according to this second passage the principle of indifference gives as a sufficient condition of truly calling alternatives equiprobable that I should be indifferent in my attitudes towards them. And if we read the first passage as being concerned with truth and not merely reasonableness of ascription of equiprobability it gives us as a sufficient condition of truly calling alternatives equiprobable, according to the principle of indifference, that we do not know that the available evidence provides a reason for preferring any one to any other. So we have two different sets of sufficient conditions for equiprobability which Kneale claims the principle of indifference to yield. It is important to see that they are different. For whatever "being indifferent in my attitudes towards two alternatives" is supposed to cover, it must surely exclude my expecting one rather than the other to be realised. But then, not knowing that the available evidence provides a reason for expecting one rather than the other is quite consistent with expecting one rather than the other. It is certainly not logically necessary that people balance their expectations when they do not know which alternative the evidence favours. For this would make one common form of having a "hunch" logically impossible. Conversely, it seems that I could be indifferent in my attitude (expect each of two things with equal confidence) even although knowing that the available evidence provides a reason for expecting one rather than the other. For the phrase "the available evidence" is properly used not just to describe the evidence which I actually have, but rather the evidence which in some sense I *could* have – I do not always avail myself of the available evidence. But then I may know that the available evidence favours one rather than the other, but, because I don't know which, (rationally) remain indifferent in my expectations. So satisfaction of one of Kneale's pair of sufficient conditions neither entails nor is entailed by satisfaction of the other.

However, there is the alternative reading of the first passage, according to which it gives conditions upon our *reasonably* calling alternatives equiprobable. This reading is perhaps more plausible if we consider the difference between Kneale's descriptions of sufficient conditions of equiprobability according to his *own* theory. From the context it appears that the respect in which alternatives should be indifferent which is referred to in the second quoted passage, is that they should cover an equal range of equipossible alternatives. So the second passage claims that a *necessary* condition of equiprobability is that the alternatives should not differ in the range of equipossibilities which they cover. Yet in the first quoted passage Kneale says that we are entitled to treat alternatives as equiprobable on his theory if we know that the available evidence does not provide a reason for preferring one to another. But then on the "truly" reading of this, Kneale has a sufficient condition for equiprobability satisfied when a necessary condition is not. For a man may know that the available evidence does not provide a reason for one rather than another, even although the alternatives are not equipossible. For there is no reason to suppose that when the alternatives are not equipossible – do not cover the same number of ultimate alternatives – the available evidence must always enable one to determine that this is so.[3]

So to preserve internal consistency, we should take Kneale to be describing, in the first passage, conditions under which according to his theory, and correspondingly according to the principle of indifference, we can reasonably say, and in that sense are entitled

[3] This is, incidentally, an excellent example of the malicious working of the objective–subjective tension described in the last chapter.

to say, that alternatives are equiprobable. It is reasonable for us to call alternatives equiprobable if we do not know that the available evidence provides a reason for preferring any one to any other.

The principle in that form cannot be true if we accept my description of the case of the biased coin where the available evidence gives no indication of the direction of bias. This case shows that the gangster and his assistant need not believe that the coin's falling heads and its falling tails are equiprobable, but indeed should positively believe the contrary, while either not knowing which the available evidence favours, or even knowing that it favours neither. There is a residual point that it may nevertheless be reasonable for them to *treat* the alternatives as equiprobable (the phrase which Kneale uses – I do not think Kneale intended to use a distinction between treating as equiprobable and believing to be equiprobable) if this simply means: expect them with equal confidence. So let us cut the knot made by introducing probability in the first place, and consider whether:

(1) We do not know, nor rationally believe, that the available evidence favours the truth of A rather than B and we do not know, nor rationally believe, that the available evidence favours the truth of B rather than A,

entails:

(2) It is unreasonable to have other than the same degree of confidence in A and B.

It is at least consistent with the spirit of Kneale's views to suppose that (1) does not entail (2), but that (2) is only entailed by the following:

(3) We do know that the available evidence does not favour the truth of A rather than B and we do know that the available evidence does not favour the truth of B rather than A.

But it is not at all evident that it is (3) rather than (1) which entails (2). It is not as though the production of (3) makes us *see* that (1) does not entail (2) and that the idea that it might results from confusing it with (3)

I am still not sure that the question of whether (1) entails (2) is *exactly* the question we want. For it is not clear why the state of ignorance which we are trying to characterise in (1) is best described in terms of ignorance of the properties of the *available evidence*. What is this concept – itself very unclear – doing in a description of a state of ignorance about two alternatives? Let us anticipate any trouble it may cause by replacing (1) with:

(4) Nothing that I know, nor rationally believe, nor should have discovered, favours A rather than B and nothing that I know, nor rationally believe, nor should have discovered, favours B rather than A.

I put in the additional clause that nothing we should have discovered favours A rather than B, nor B rather than A, to take care of the point raised in chapter 2, that irrationality may arise from negligence to rectify a state of ignorance as well as from misuse of knowledge.

(2) is framed negatively in order to avoid a hollow acceptance of the entailment. If (2) was simply put as "it is reasonable to have the same degree of confidence in A and B", we would run the risk of accepting the entailment simply because (4) puts no constraints on what it is rational to believe. That is, a complete sceptic might say that (4) entails that it is reasonable to have the same degree of confidence in A and in B – also reasonable to have, say, twice as much confidence in A as in B, and in fact reasonable to distribute our confidence in whatever way we fancy. If the sceptic was right (4) would not entail (2), however. The question of whether it does is, I think, identical with the question of whether another slightly simpler entailment holds. (4) it will be noted is a conjunction. Now (2) can be represented as a conjunction: 'It is unreasonable to have more confidence in A than in B and it is unreasonable to have more confidence in B than in A.' It is quite clear then that the question of whether the conjunction (4) entails the conjunction (2) is just the question of whether the corresponding conjuncts entail each other. That is, being ignorant as described in (4) of anything favouring A rather than B and of anything favouring B rather than A will entail being constrained to have no more confidence in A rather than B nor in B rather than A *if and only if* being ignorant as described in (4) of anything favouring A rather than B entails being constrained to have no more confidence in A than B. So we now ask whether:

(5) Nothing that I know, nor rationally believe, nor should have discovered, favours A rather than B

entails:

> (6) It is unreasonable for me to have more confidence in A than in B

For good measure there is a final reduction of *this* very simple question to another. Contraposing, it becomes the problem of whether:

> (7) It is only reasonable for me to have more confidence in A than in B

entails:

> (8) There is something which I know, or rationally believe, or should have discovered, which favours A rather than B.

It is at first sight surprising that we can reduce the discussion of a form of the principle of indifference to this question. The reduction is perhaps the more surprising in that it is by no means obvious that (7) does not entail (8), nor that (4) does not entail (2). And these questions are perhaps nearer the point of Bernoulli's formulation, saying that we should expect alternatives equally "quia nulla perspicitur ratio cur haec vel illa potius exire debeat quam quaelibet alia",[4] than formulations using the concept of probability and available evidence.

Objections

The classical argument against any form of the principle of indifference is that unless the alternatives A and B are restricted in some way, the principle leads to absurdity and even contradiction. Thus it is thought that Bernoulli's maxim would lead as surely to having the same confidence that 'not-6' (i.e. 1 or 2 or 3 or 4 or 5) will fall on a die as that 6 will – and to the same confidence that 5 will fall as that 6 will. The conclusion is drawn that a requirement of the equispecificity in some sense of A and B must be imposed. However it seems to be doubtful whether in cases like this the requirement of equispecificity is an additional requirement to the condition that (4) must be true for an application of the principle. That is, if the alternatives are not reasonably thought to be equispecific it is doubtful whether (4) is true in any case. For example,

---

[4] "Because no reason is to be seen why this or that should be the outcome rather than any other one you care to mention." Bernoulli, *Ars Conjectandi*, 1713, Pt IV, p. 224. Quoted in Kneale, p. 147.

suppose that we have two people, both entirely ignorant about the size of a population of bacteria in a test-tube. A scientist tells them that it lies between five million and seven million, but tells them no more. Consider four hypotheses:

(P) The population is between 5,000,000 and 6,000,000
(Q) The population is between 6,000,000 and 7,000,000
(R) The population is between 6,500,000 and 7,000,000
(S) The population is between 6,000,000 and 6,500,000

(Q) is identical with the disjunction (R) or (S). The question we have to ask is whether accepting that (4) entails (2) involves accepting the grossly implausible supposition that it is reasonable to have the same degree of confidence in (P) as in (R), or in (Q) as in (S). It does not seem to me to do so. For consider the comparison, in this situation of ignorance, between (Q) and (R). Is it true that nothing that I know, nor rationally believe, nor should have discovered, favours (Q) rather than (R)? I should have thought not. For one thing I know is that (Q) is identical with the disjunction (R) or (S). So it is reasonable to have the same degree of confidence in (Q) as in (R) if and only if it is reasonable to have no confidence at all in (S). Only if it is right to be certain that the population is not in the first half of the interval, is it right to have the same confidence that it is in the second half of the interval as that it lies in the interval at all. So even in this situation of ignorance in which the scientist leaves us, we have a good reason for putting more confidence in (Q) than in (R), namely that we have no right to be certain that (S) is false. Indeed, precisely since (R) and (S) satisfy the premiss (4) it is right according to the principle to expect each equally and thence put twice as much confidence in (Q), and hence, using the principle again, in (P), as in either of them. Similarly with the die example. A reason can be seen for having more confidence in the disjunctive hypothesis (1 or 2 or 3 or 4 or 5 will fall), than in the hypothesis that 5 will fall, namely that it is not certain that none of 1, 2, 3 or 4 will fall; so if, as is admitted, no reason can be seen why 5 rather than 6 or 6 rather than 5 should fall, then more reason can be seen why (1 or 2 or 3 or 4 or 5) should be expected than 6.

A more serious limitation on the use of the principle arises when we try to use it in estimating the confidence we should have in the value of a certain measurement being within a certain interval. For here there can be an arbitrariness affecting the division of the total possible range into alternatives which could, apparently, yield different and incompatible alternatives each claiming a right to the same degree of confidence. Thus the specific volume of a substance is the reciprocal of its specific density. If we know only that a specific volume lies between 1 and 3 we might use the principle that (4) entails (2) to justify our having equal confidence that it lies between 1 and 2 and that it lies between 2 and 3, and to attack any other distribution of confidence as irrational. But we can describe our evidence equally well as telling us that the specific density lies between 1 and $\frac{1}{3}$, so it would be as plausible to use the principle to give us equal confidence that this lies between 1 and $\frac{2}{3}$ and between $\frac{2}{3}$ and $\frac{1}{3}$. But this is logically equivalent to saying that it is right to have equal confidence that the specific volume lies between 1 and $1\frac{1}{2}$ and between $1\frac{1}{2}$ and 3: conflicting with the first claim, that the ranges 1 to 2 and 2 to 3 deserve equal confidence.

Quite generally, for any measure of a physical property a function can be constructed on m with values f(m), such that where $m_1 < m_2 < m_3 < m_4$:

$$\frac{m_3 - m_2}{m_4 - m_1} \neq \frac{f(m_3) - f(m_2)}{f(m_4) - f(m_1)}$$

In particular then, although the expression on the left-hand side may equal $\frac{1}{2}$, the expression on the right-hand side may equal anything at all, depending on the choice of the function f. The question then arises: how can the principle that (4) entails (2) *either* avoid inconsistency *or* be used to determine one right distribution of confidence, i.e. select one function f such that, when $f(m_2) - f(m_3) = \frac{1}{2}(f(m_4) - f(m_1))$, it is right to have confidence that the value of the physical quality lies between m_2 and m_3 which is one-half of the confidence that it lies in the total range m_1 to m_4?

Lord Keynes's masterly presentation of this problem puts it thus:

"The objective quality measured may not, strictly speaking, possess numerical quantitativeness, although it has the properties necessary for measurement by means of correlation with numbers. The values which it can assume may be capable of being ranged in an order. . .but it does not follow from this that there is any meaning in the assertion that one value is twice another value. . .It follows that equal intervals between the numbers which represent the ratios do not necessarily correspond to equal intervals between the qualities under measurement; for these numerical differences depend upon which convention of measurement we have selected."[5]

However, it is a mistake to think that the problem arises only with properties that do not possess "numerical quantitativeness", as the first sentence seems to suggest. If this were so, we could perhaps hope that the argument demonstrated an incompleteness in the use of the principle that (4) entails (2) rather than an inconsistency. But in fact the full dress argument for inconsistency can be carried out using as an example a property which has a paradigmatic numerical quantitativeness, namely the population of a set. To adapt the example of the scientist with his population of bacteria slightly, we have:

Premiss (*1*): The population lies between 6 and 9 (units of some sort)
   (a) It lies between 6 and 7
   (b) It lies between 7 and 8
   (c) It lies between 8 and 9
   (4_{abc}): Nothing that I know, nor rationally believe, nor should have discovered, favours any of (a), (b) or (c) against the others.

Principle: (4) entails (2). Therefore:

   (2_{abc}): It is unreasonable to have other than the same degree of confidence in each of (a) and (b) and (c).

From (1): The reciprocal of the population lies between $1/6$ and $1/9$, i.e. between $6/54$ and $9/54$.
   (d) It lies between $6/54$ and $7/54$
   (e) It lies between $7/54$ and $8/54$
   (f) It lies between $8/54$ and $9/54$
   (4_{def}): Nothing that I know, nor rationally believe, nor should have discovered, favours any of (d), (e) or (f) against the others.

Principle: (4) entails (2). Therefore:

   (2_{def}): It is unreasonable to have other than the same degree of confidence in each of (d), (e) and (f).
   (3) (f) is logically equivalent to (g): the population lies between

[5] Keynes, *Treatise on Probability*, p. 46.

6 and 6¾; (e) to (h): the population lies between 6¾ and 7⁵⁄₇; (d) to (i): the population lies between 7⁵⁄₇ and 9.

(2_{ghi}): It is unreasonable to have other than the same degree of confidence in each of (g), (h) and (i).

But each triplet a, b, c; d, e, f; g, h, i; exhausts the possibilities. So:

(5) It is unreasonable to have other than the same degree of confidence (namely one third) in (a) and in (g).

But (5) is true if and only if it is reasonable to have no confidence that the population lies between 6¾ and 7. But another use of the principle will clearly assure us that it is *un*reasonable to have no confidence that the population lies between 6¾ and 7. The principle therefore leads to contradiction.

Clearly the only hope for a way out of this argument is to deny that where (4_{abc}) is true, (4_{def}) is also true. And this might seem plausible by in effect contraposing the argument: if no reason can be seen for distinguishing (a), (b) and (c), then a jolly good reason can be seen for distinguishing (d), (e) and (f), namely that if we don't we are inconsistent. But the force of the argument is missed by the manoeuvre, for we now ask: granted that we cannot hold both (4_{abc}) and (4_{def}), what principle have we to tell us which one we should give up? How does someone who thinks that (4_{abc}) is true argue with someone who thinks that (4_{def}) is true, remembering that all the scientist has told us is given in the premiss (1), and that nothing else is known about the population?

I know of no direct answer to this question. But we can remark that in an enormous variety of cases, and perhaps all, we naturally and unanimously take the proportion of a population covered in an hypothesis such as (a) as the measure of the degree of confidence which it is right to have in it. For example all of us, were we to be on a mountain in a fog, would prefer it to be a mountain in which most directions lead to safety than one in which most directions lead to destruction. Further examples can be constructed ad lib, but by themselves they give no insight into the rationality of our propensity. We are still offered no reason for taking (4_{abc}) as true, and (4_{def}) as consequently false. In the next section I shall offer a clarification of our propensity and the principle which we appear to use, and we can then approach nearer to the justification of it. For the present then the situation is that we offer the principle that (4) entails (2), which is equivalent to the even more plausible looking principle that (5) entails (6). The trouble then arises that if we do not exercise great care in deciding when (4) is true, and in particular if we do not choose just one of the many mutually consistent ways of describing the alternatives A and B for which (4) might be supposed true, then contradiction arises. I now claim that although in general I can see no way of supplementing the principle by a device for making such a choice, in the particular case where the hypotheses concern proportions of populations with a certain characteristic we make the choice naturally and unanimously. We can now turn to trying to clarify, and, it is to be hoped, to justify, this propensity.

Proportions

The principle I am going to maintain I shall call the Population Indifference Principle, PIP. It may be regarded as a restriction of the principle that (4) entails (2) to a case in which (4) is true for a particular reason, and is stated as follows:

If (i) A thing x is known to belong to a set S, *and*
   (ii) A and B are known to be two numerically equal subsets of S, *and*
  (iii) Nothing further relevant to determining whether x is an A or x is a B is known, nor rationally believed, nor should have been discovered,

then it follows that:
  (iv) It is unreasonable to have other than the same confidence that x is an A as that x is a B.

As a corollary to this we can derive the principle which is of more direct use in the enquiry, the Majority Indifference Principle, MIP. It is stated as follows:

If (i) A thing x is known to belong to a set S, *and*
  (ii) It is known that more members of S are members of A than are members of B, *and*
  (iii) Nothing further relevant to determining whether x is an A or x is a B is known, nor rationally believed, nor should have been discovered,

then it follows that:
  (iv) It is unreasonable to have other than more confidence that x is an A than that x is a B.

The most common application of this has B $= \sim$A; (ii) then means that most Ss are A. MIP is derivable from PIP, for by PIP if A has more members than B, it will be obligatory to have the same confidence that x is a B as that x is a member of any proper subset of A containing as many members as B. Then dividing A into n nonintersecting equinumerous proper subsets, the union of m of which is equinumerous with B, it will be obligatory to have n times the degree of confidence that x is an A as that x is a member of any one such subset, m times the degree of confidence that x is a B as that x is a member of any one such subset, and so n/m times the confidence that x is an A as that x is a B.

I shall firstly describe how PIP differs from a much weaker principle, i.e. one demanding a further premiss for the entailment. The point of considering this weaker principle is that it appears to do two things. It appears to offer a direct connection with success – with obtaining true belief. But it buys the advantage by reintroducing the concept of objective probability. I shall then argue that we must accept PIP and not the weaker principle, and finally I shall show the extreme diffculty of giving PIP anything other than a fundamental status, i.e. the difficulty of deriving it from any other considerations governing reasoning.

The weaker principle in question would demand that something further should be known about x in order to yield (iv), namely that x should have been chosen from the set S by a method random with respect to selection of As and Bs. If for example we are faced with a bag of balls of which say 99 per cent are white and the remainder black, and know absolutely nothing about a ball x except that it is in the bag, use of MIP dictates that we should have extremely high confidence that the ball is white. The weaker principle would demand that we should know in addition that x is selected by means of a method which is not biased in favour of black balls.

If we do not know this we might try arguing that symmetry considerations show that of all the biased methods that might be used to pick out x, exactly the same number would be biased towards black as white balls; so, knowing nothing about it, it is equally reasonable to suppose that the method used favours white as black. The trouble with this is that it depends upon the same move as that in question: it depends upon our knowledge that an equal proportion of methods favour white as favour black, and knowing nothing else relevant about the method used to select x, together entailing that it is reasonable to have identical confidence that white will be favoured and that black will. The protagonist of knowledge of randomness will not be impressed by this: he would say that this would only follow if the method used to pick out x had been chosen at random from the total number of possible methods. So the argument remains the same whether we introduce consideration of methods of selection or not.

Why should anyone urge the necessity of the randomness premiss? The answer lies in success: if you say that x is white knowing that x was selected by a *fair method* you will be right, it is hoped, *most* of the time if most of the balls are white, or at any rate you would so be right "in the long run". Whereas not knowing that x is selected by a fair method you could be wrong most of the time however long the run, for there is no guarantee or assessable probability that when (i), (iii), and the proposition that most Ss are A are true, *most* answers that x is A would be correct even "in the long run". So if reasoning is to be concerned with success in producing truths – and we saw in chapter 2 that this is fundamental to its meaning – the randomness premiss must be added.

Hacking has argued that the "success in the long run" justification cannot be used to found a particular case of having confidence that a ball is white.[6] His argument is based upon Peirce's point that we will put confidence in the hypothesis that x is white when we know that it is chosen at random from a bag containing 99 per cent white balls and 1 per cent black even if we know that there is going to be no opportunity for us (or perhaps anybody else) to indulge in a long run of guesses on this matter (or perhaps on anything else). We would be right to guess white if a correct guess meant a nice death as opposed to a nasty one for all sentient beings. I confess that I am not clear about the force of this objection to the long run justification. For Peirce describes a situation in which there will be no long run of guesses. But the long run justification finds the reason for our being right to guess white in the fact that *if* there were a long run of such guesses most *would be* correct, and that proposition may remain true even if there isn't actually going to be a long run of guesses. Hacking's reply would be, presumably, that if we know there isn't going to be such a long run of guesses, why should we take into account the fact that if there were one, most would be

[6] Hacking, *Logic of Statistical Inference*, ch. IV, pp. 42–51.

successful? I am not sure why we should, but it seems to be possible that we should. The situation may be compared with moral praise. 'If everybody did as he did, the world would be a better place' can be a commendation when we know that the conditional will not be fulfilled and when we also know that his particular action was unfortunate, as when he lost his life in a futile act of mercy.

However the important point here is not whether this sort of defence against the Hacking/Peirce argument could be successful. The important question is what any argument which seeks to introduce the randomness premiss from long run considerations must be based upon. For the basic argument appears to be: (a) this guess is a member of a long run of (potential) guesses, and (b) most guesses in that long run are correct, and (c) nothing further is known, rationally believed, or should have been discovered, about this guess, *so* it is right to have confidence in this guess. But this form of argument is precisely that which was condemned as invalid by the probabilist; for the issue between a supporter of MIP and him is that he thinks a further premiss is needed for any such inference. In this case, has he got that premiss? The further premiss has to be, in place of (c), that the particular guess is chosen at random, or by a method fair with respect to the truth or falsity of the guess chosen. But where on earth can *that* premiss come from? This particular guess is the one we are interested in: it is not "chosen" from a long run of possible guesses by any method at all, let alone one which preserves equal probability of true or false guesses being selected. Of course (c) is true of it, but according to the attacker of MIP that is not good enough.

So we cannot both attack MIP and present a long run type of justification of the demand for a stronger premiss. But there is I think a more fundamental point than this in the offing, which is that in the absence of MIP it is doubtful whether knowledge of the randomness of a method of selection could ever be claimed anyway, in a sense strong enough to give an alternative to MIP. For consider what sort of situation the probabilist is envisaging. We are drawing with replacement[7] from a bag of balls 99 per cent of which are white, 1 per cent of which are black. When a particular ball has been picked the probabilist only allows us to place more confidence in white than black if we know or rationally believe that the method

[7] This means: so that the constitution of the bag is the same on each subsequent draw.

of selection is not biased with respect to colour of ball picked. Now how do we obtain that knowledge about a particular method of selection? By performing a long series of tests, and finding that over a sufficient period the method selects balls in no significant order and in proportion to the number in the set from which selection is made. There is then an inference to the proposition that the method *does* do this, from the evidence that it *has* done it on the series of tests. The strength of this inference is the strength of:

(Q) If the method were biased it would have given different results on the long series of tests.

Why accept (Q)? The answer lies in:

(R) If the method were biased it would give different results on *nearly all* such long series of tests.

(Making precise the "nearly all" "long series" in quantified terms is a task of the statistical theory of testing.)

But what is the nature of the inference from the knowledge that a biased method would fail (be detected) over most such series, to the supposition that it would be detected on this one? Again we have the premisses for an argument of the form of MIP, but no stronger argument.

Finally the most powerful argument against the probabilist arises if we ask what he does with the conclusion that the method selects 99 per cent white and 1 per cent black balls in no significant order. For do we not merely change the set S under consideration? Instead of 'The ball comes from a set of 99 per cent white and 1 per cent black balls, and nothing further is known, rationally believed, or should have been discovered about it', we get: 'The ball comes from the set of balls selected from a bag by a method which produces 99 per cent white and 1 per cent black in no significant order, and nothing further is known, etc., about it.' But again the inference from the second proposition to the irrationality of having other than 99 per cent confidence that the ball is white is not conspicuously better than the inference from the first. Both depend upon MIP.

In sum it appears impossible to produce a probabilistic theory of distributing confidence according to proportions which does not covertly argue in accordance with PIP or MIP at some point. Still, it might be asked, do we use or need PIP in empirical reasoning, or can we do without any such principle? I think all that I can do is point to the numerous sorts of argument which depend upon PIP, and to the impossibility of saying anything at all about rational expectation without it.

Reasoning with PIP and MIP

The preceding defence of these principles against the necessity of a probabilistic weakening will, if successful, convince us that they underlie a great deal of our empirical reasoning. There are other, more obvious cases in which they appear to be used. There are the philosophers' constructed cases: wouldn't you bet on white if you had to choose the colour of a ball about which you knew nothing except that it came from a set 99.999 per cent of which are white, if horrible consequences follow a mistake? But without constructing special examples, we can see the principle at work throughout everyday life. I am reasonable in hiring a car of make X rather than make Y if all I know is that cars of make X generally get there, whereas cars of make Y generally don't. If most eggs from source X are known to be bad, but virtually no eggs from source Y, and I know nothing about this egg except its origin, I am more foolish to crack it straight into my omelette if it is an X egg than if it is a Y egg. And so on.

There is a very neat connection between PIP and MIP on the one hand and our analysis of reasoning given in chapter 2 on the other. Consider the three premisses of MIP. The third premiss, (iii), assures us that we neither have nor should have countervailing evidence about x. So if the first two provide a reason for supposing that x is an A rather than a B, the addition of the third will give a situation in which it is reasonable to suppose that x is an A rather than a B. Now according to the analysis of chapter 2 the question of whether the first two premisses provide a reason for supposing that x is an A rather than a B is in effect the question of whether:

> If our confidence is to be adjusted in a way which generally furthers accord with the truth, then it is right to have more confidence that x is an A rather than a B upon coming to know that x is a member of a set containing more As than Bs.

And whenever (iii) is true, so that we are ignorant of factors which might make x likely to be an A or likely not to be an A, this proposition will be true. Because one would be right more often, over the generality of cases, to expect x to be A, precisely because more members of the set S are As than are Bs.

It is necessary to realise that "one would be right more often, over the generality of cases..." does not mean that one *will* be right more often, even in a long run of cases. It means that in general, presented with an x from such a set, it is relatively rare for it to be a B. The policy of aiming at the truth therefore dictates increased confidence in x being A, for this is the more common truth.

We are now, I think, right at the bedrock of justification. On p. 34 I raised the possibility of a sceptic who, although he wanted to get at the truth on a particular occasion, announced himself indifferent to the unreasonable nature of some belief. Because, he said, reasoning may yield a false belief. All that reasoning is analysed as doing is generally furthering accord with the truth. So where is the objection to neglecting it on occasion? Well, we can say, our analysis of reason shows MIP to be a good argument. This our sceptic admits, for it was not the analysis that he objected to, it was the propriety of criticising him as unreasonable if that was what the concept amounted to. So, we continue, we can use MIP as follows: since reasoning generally furthers accord with the truth, most unreasonable beliefs are false, nothing further is known etc. about his unreasonable belief, therefore it is unreasonable to place confidence in his belief. But this is peculiarly limp, because the sceptic has already announced himself to be indifferent to this conclusion. All that we have done is "back up" the conclusion by presenting a connection between what is generally the case and what is reasonable on occasion. The sceptic can, and must, admit this, but need not worry, because he is indifferent to this sort of conclusion about particular cases anyway.

In short, the concept of reason may be such as to assure the validity of MIP. But the use of the concept of reason to criticise a particular belief or argument is proper because of MIP. It gives us no leverage against someone who doubts the relevance of what is generally the case to what is the case on the occasion in which he is interested. So we can say that the application of reason and belief in MIP stand or fall together, but neither could properly be said to justify the other. It is however possible to remark that we do think it a criticism of a particular belief to say that it is unreasonable, and that we do regard it as a criticism to say of the sceptic who announces himself indifferent to the results of a policy which generally furthers accord with the truth, that he is generally wrong.

These things, in addition to the examples I gave above, underline the extent of our commitment to MIP. Another extremely important area in which this emerges is the following. Consider the notion of a *policy* for prediction. Suppose that an enquiry into the rationality of induction was successful enough to show that over a period of time most expectations in accordance with some policy would be successful. This would be an impressive result certainly. It would give us the right to say that if our confidence is to be distributed in a way which generally furthers accord with the truth, (this sort of) I-evidence must raise our confidence in (this sort of) I-prediction. I-evidence is a reason for an I-prediction (of this sort). But if a sceptic then announced himself, on an occasion, indifferent to the production of this sort of evidence, all that we could reply would be that on most occasions like this the belief which is linked to the evidence is true, nothing further is known, etc., about this occasion, so the uniquely reasonable expectation is that the sceptic is wrong. But if we think MIP is a bad argument, we cannot say that. And if we cannot say that, we are left with absolutely no criticism of somebody who is prepared to regard the general success of a policy as irrelevant whenever it suits him.

Any theory of induction must realise that there remains a problem if all that is achieved is a comparison of policies. Suppose for example we took the view that any counter-inductive policy is in some way inconsistent, i.e. leads to contradictory results. This would not by itself amount to a justification of induction – a proof that we are right to have confidence in appropriately backed I-predictions. For if we take the negation of any such I-prediction, how are we to derive the irrationality of having confidence in *that*? Even if the policy of expecting change is inconsistent if it is applied indiscriminately, still I do not contradict myself if I arbitrarily announce that I expect my typewriter to change colour within the next five seconds.

I have now said enough about the nature of our principles, and the place that they, or something similar, must play in any theory of rational belief. What then of the inconsistency which unrestricted use of such principles yields? Inconsistency arises because until we are forewarned we think that the "nothing further relevant..." condition is satisfied in too many cases. Now there can be genuine empirical disagreement about the satisfaction of this condition. For example suppose that I am given two books and told that one of them is "foxed" by having brown spotting on one page. I may find the "nothing further relevant..." condition satisfied, and have the same confidence that one is foxed as that the other is. But then we find that one book has ninety pages and the other has ten. Is that relevant? There is scope for disagreement here. One bibliophile might believe that if a book is foxed it is always foxed on its first page, and that a book's propensity to fox is independent of its size. He regards the further information as irrelevant. Whereas a rival might think that any particular page is as susceptible to fox as any other, regardless of how they are assorted into books, and he has premisses to give him great confidence that the bigger book is foxed. Which of these is likely to be right is then a matter for librarians, not philosophers. My defence of the use of the "nothing further relevant..." condition that we shall need has in effect been three-fold: we all use it naturally and unanimously; no statistical theory could avoid it; and it is sufficiently intertwined with the very concept of a reason to justify it. When, for example, we condemn a particular argument because it is a sort which usually gives the wrong answer, and nothing further relevant is known about its use on this occasion, it would be feeble to use the existence of Keynes's type of problem to escape the charge. We would rightly demand something genuinely relevant, and that would be something which distinguishes the use on this occasion, and puts it into a higher success bracket than its untrustworthy type generally merits.

Before turning to the daunting problem of describing an inductive policy which gives the premisses for the use of our principles, we may notice one small point in passing, namely that PIP vindicates the assumption made in chapter 3, that confidence should be distributed according to proportions, in the absence of countervailing knowledge. This vindicates the arguments adapted from Carnap showing the general difficulty of tying the logic of the dyadic relation 'R' to that of entailment.

I showed at the end of chapter 4 that the problem is well represented diagrammatically; justify putting confidence in a straight hypothesis rather than any of the unlimited number of kinked, differentiating courses. We remarked that most of the differentiating hypotheses had to be false, because of their mutual inconsistency. We now have a principle which entitles us to criticise the placing of confidence in any one of them. For, to take the example of the colour of the lawn, if we select an hypothesis that the lawn will undergo a *particular* change at a *particular* time, then if nothing is known, rationally believed, or should have been discovered, justifying that choice of values, all we know is that the hypothesis is a member of a set of hypotheses the vast majority of which must be false. And by the use of MIP we deduce that it is irrational to place much confidence in a proposition when all that is known about it is that it keeps such bad company.

This negative result is grist to a sceptic's mill, of course, for he makes the now familiar move that all that is known about the straight hypothesis is that it keeps the same bad company. So if MIP is to provide a ground for more ambitious results a way must be found to show that a particular case of selection of a straight hypothesis is a member of some class of selections with a high success rate. So to proceed further we must address the question of whether an inductive policy could be described whereby most I-propositions relating in the way it requires to the I-evidence must be true. And this would be declared by many to be absolutely impossible. It is however premature to despair at this demand. It may be that our analytical exertions have just given us a magnificent view of the impossibility of the problem, long suspected. But in the next chapter I shall show that this is not so, and that using some equipment left by a previous attempt we can at least reach a minor summit.

7

Successful policies

An argument of Sir Roy Harrod's

It is perfectly obvious that any policy of reasoning which can be proved to be generally successful must be fairly unambitious. If, when provided with a little limited knowledge about what a bit of the world is like, we immediately trust in an enormous extrapolation to embrace all other bits of the world at all places and all times, no assurance of general success will be forthcoming. It is no wonder that philosophers, listening only to the great rolling universal quantifiers which they believe that scientists dictate, throw up the whole business, and counsel us instead to trust in what is simple, or falsifiable – these things having then no visible connection at all with what is true. It can then be suggested that Science need not bother about truth, but is instead searching for elegance, or excitement, or whatever. Well, perhaps it is, but the ordinary man is concerned not with all time and space, but with what is going to happen when he takes an aspirin or goes into a room or trusts his weight to a rope or lights the gas. And by "concerned with what is going to happen" we mean concerned with whether certain expectations are *true*, not with whether they are elegant, or daring. Unfortunately, philosophers have seldom combined the point that we are concerned with general success, with the awareness that we are entitled to look at unambitious, small, extrapolations from experience.

In his book Harrod gives what he considers to be a conclusive argument, from inevitable success, for the rationality of expecting uniformities to continue a certain way given *solely* that they have continued for a certain time.[1] This would be an argument for having great confidence in the second sort of I-proposition given solely the appropriate I-evidence. The argument is conducted in terms of the high probability of some such predictions, but is easily transferred to a demonstration that it is rational to have a great deal of confidence in them.

---

[1] Harrod, *Foundations of Inductive Logic*, 1956, ch. 3.

The argument is presented thus:

"We are starting, as we must in a fundamental analysis of induction, from a condition of total nescience...Consider a journey by such a nescient man along a continuity. The continuity may consist of a uniform colour, texture or sound, or of a repeated pattern, where the pattern is easily cognizable at a glance, this uniformity being in contrast with a heterogeneous background...Let a conclusion be proposed that this continuity will continue for a length constituting at least one-tenth of the length for which it has already proceeded. In more general terms we may suppose belief in a continuance for at least $1/x$ of the length for which it has already proceeded. If we entertain the belief of at least one-tenth, which is the conclusion of our argument, continuously from the beginning to the end of the journey, it is quite certain that we shall be right ten times for every once that we are wrong. We shall be right during the first ten-elevenths of the journey, and wrong during the last eleventh. If we entertain the belief of continuance for at least $1/x$, it is quite certain that we shall be right x times for every once that we are wrong. This in accordance with the traditional notation, gives a probability of being correct of $x/(x+1)$. The probability of the belief in continuance will be higher, the more modest the extrapolation.[2]

This is an attempt to provide a description of a way of reasoning which has exactly the feature which we want: applied over a period of time, it must have a high success rate. It is therefore of the greatest importance to determine what value could be attached to this argument, and correspondingly strange that the literature should contain so little notice of it. The only attempts to refute it that I can find occur in Bronowski, Popper, and Kyburg:[3] between them they muster three arguments against Harrod's view, and there are hints of a fourth in the first two articles. These arguments represent many people's initial reaction to this strange argument, so I shall begin by treating them quite fully.

[2] Harrod, pp. 52–3.
[3] Bronowski, "The Scandal of Philosophy", *B.J.P.S.*, 1957; Popper, "Mr. Harrod on Induction", *B.J.P.S.*, 1958; Kyburg, "Recent Work in Inductive Logic", *American Philosophical Quarterly*, 1964.

Bronowski's argument is that "Mr Harrod begins by making his imagery, and ends by making his reasoning, hinge on the properties of space as we know it." Harrod "pictures the progress of his nescient man as a journey; and if this picture is to be universal, then the journey must be not in a space but in something more general and abstract – we can call it an experience-space. Mr Harrod silently assumes that this abstract experience-space has the same properties as the Euclidean space in which we move physically." Other spaces might "quite distort his succession of fractional steps", or be "fissured everywhere by discontinuities". Kyburg accepts this objection, and expresses it by saying that other spaces might have "more fence per pasture".

Neither of these writers say anything more about the relevance of considering non-Euclidean spaces. Now it is true that Harrod's argument is readily expressible in spatial terms, and indeed the passage quoted phrases the whole view in terms of a journey along a continuity. A natural example to use is of two people in a car crossing a desert and discussing the probable continuation of the desert. But if we forego this example it is readily apparent that the talk of a journey is really a metaphor detachable from the core of the argument. Harrod is concerned with the position of anybody who has experienced a regularity – an object having a property, a sensation continuing, an extremely general law holding – for a certain time, and wondering whether it will continue for some further time expressible as a fraction of its known duration. Now to be aware of continuity is not to make a journey through our space, nor indeed any other space. It may, perversely, be described as making a journey through an "experience-space" where this phrase is given its sense by the identity: to have journeyed through as S-filled part of experience-space for ten minutes is to have been aware of S for ten minutes. Even so, the only dimension along which I travel if I sit with a pain in my head for ten minutes is that of time. If we prefer to say that I took ten minutes to cross a headache-filled expanse of experience-space, then we must remember that no sense has been given to talk of the metric of this space, of its containing straight lines, curved lines, parallel lines or angles; *a fortiori* no sense is given to supposing that it in any way conforms or fails to conform to Euclidean geometry. So this objection is totally incoherent, and it is no accident that neither writer tries to show how the translation into terms of "experience-space" is to cast doubt upon the analyticity that one-tenth of the duration of a finite regularity occurs in the last tenth of its life.

Popper puts Harrod's point in terms of a betting contract. Peter and Paul are aware of a continuity, and enter into the following contract. Peter owes Paul $x/(x+1)$ pennies if the continuity ends in the next m/x minutes, where m is its duration so far, and x is any number. If the end is not reached in that time Paul owes Peter $1/(x+1)$ pennies. If they start at the beginning of the continuity, and if the time interval of these bets is small compared to the total life of the continuity, then they will be square at its end. "The odds of x to 1 in favour of not reaching the end in m/x minutes were fair odds. Therefore the probability of not doing so is $x/(x+1)$."[4] Popper then points out that this contract to bet regularly at these odds remains fair, even if either Peter or Paul or both knows exactly when the end of the desert will be reached. So, says Popper, "the probability cannot be a probability that may be interpreted as the degree of Peter or Paul's imperfect knowledge". The "probability" calculated, concludes Popper, is nothing but the proportion of games Peter is bound to win.

Although the features of the betting contract that Popper points out are interesting and possibly important, the difficulty is in seeing how they refute Harrod's argument. Harrod replies to Popper by citing a parallel situation.[5] Peter and Paul, incorrigible but safe gamblers, agree that one should pay the other a penny if a black card turns up, and vice versa if a red card turns up, as they run through a pack which they know to be complete and correct. Betting thus at even odds on the emergence of a black card they are again certain to be all square at the end of the performance. Again, the fairness of the contract is unaffected by any additional knowledge that either of them may possess, e.g. about the actual order of the cards in the pack. But if we take this as showing that the probability of a card drawn under these circumstances being black is $\frac{1}{2}$, Popper would have to say that we have made a mistake. He would have to say that this figure cannot be interpreted as a probability: $\frac{1}{2}$, he would conclude, is nothing but the proportion of the games that Peter is bound to win. But, as Harrod rightly says, $\frac{1}{2}$ *is* the proportion of games that

[4] Popper, p. 233.
[5] Harrod, "The New Argument for Induction: Reply to Professor Popper", *B.J.P.S.*, 1959.

someone is bound to win, but what is remarkable about that is that it can be laid down *a priori*, and what Popper has failed to show is why the proportion of games that somebody is bound to win should not also be interpreted as the probability of the sort of thing he is betting on. Certainly, if nothing further is known, rationally believed, or should have been found out, about the result of one particular bet in this series, MIP would apply to show us that Peter is right to have confidence that the continuity will not end. The question is whether the antecedent is satisfied.

In addition to condoning Bronowski's argument, Kyburg offers one of his own:

> "The 'next' n/x ft after I have travelled n ft [Kyburb is considering the case in which the continuity is represented by an expanse over which I am making a journey] is not a random member of the set of x + 1 intervals with respect to revealing a discontinuity, because I already have knowledge that there is no discontinuity in the first x intervals. If there is a discontinuity at all it must be in the (x + 1)th interval. The probability that there is no discontinuity in the (x + 1)th interval, given that there is none in the first x, is just the probability, a priori, that there is no discontinuity in the first x + 1 intervals. We have no way of calculating this, but equally we have no way to be sure that it is as small as Mr. Harrod would like it to be."[6]

This is an altogether more formidable argument. The point that the next interval is not a random member of the set of intervals with respect to revealing a discontinuity, because it is known that there was none in the first x intervals, will turn up to cast a shadow over any account of Harrod's argument which presents it as a straightforward use of MIP. I shall have much more to say about it later. But the rest of Kyburg's objection seems too strong. We can freely admit that degrees of confidence should obey the probability axioms. But in chapter 5 we saw some of the dangers of putting the matter in terms of objective probabilities of which we can too easily be thought to be ignorant. Kyburg seems to think that we could only be justified in attaching a high degree of confidence to the prediction if we knew something (the probability of the continuity ending within x + 1 intervals) *a priori*. He himself points out that we have

[6] Kyburg, p. 262.

no way of calculating this, and it is no wonder, since the demand would be that we "calculate" the value of this probability out of total nescience. But the right moral to draw is just one of scepticism about the existence of this figure, whose value dictates everything about rational expectation, but which can't conceivably be calculated.

The last objection which I wish to mention, primarily because I think it tempts many people who hear Harrod's position for the first time, is given characteristic expression by Bronowski:

> "Mr Harrod's procedure is certainly not universal. Consider for example a man's progress through his own life. Mr Harrod invites him to plan at 20 on the assumption that he will live for another two years. But if the man survives to 80 Mr Harrod asks him to plan the rest of his life on the assumption that he will live for another eight years. Even the nescient man would sense that this policy, however human, is not reasonable."[7]

Another version of the same objection is that Harrod's argument, if correct, should lead one to believe that the further a car goes without a refill of petrol, the more likely it is to travel another ten miles without a refill. But the short reply is that Harrod is concerned with the probability of continuance *simply* upon the evidence of past continuation. There is nothing in his argument which precludes him from taking into account, in any empirical situation, other evidence *against* future continuations, such as the fact that most men die before they reach ages much above eighty, or that cars need petrol. And, of course, at best this point could only be that the conclusion is unacceptable, it still does not show what is wrong with Harrod's method of getting there.

It is now time to start my own analysis of the argument. What is absolutely certain is that the following proposition is true:

(T) If a man entertains and believes the proposition that a regularity will continue for at least one-tenth as long again as its previous duration, at regular intervals, small compared to the total length of the continuity from (very near to) the beginning to the end of the continuity, he will be right in at least ten-elevenths of his beliefs.

[7] Bronowski, p. 330.

In fact, he will be right in exactly ten-elevenths of his beliefs if the continuity does at some point end. If it goes on for ever, he will be always right.

(T) is a tautology, for the man will be right until the last eleventh of the life of the regularity, which time will contain, under the conditions laid down, exactly one-eleventh of his beliefs about its life. The question is one of the route from (T) to any interesting proposition about what it is reasonable to expect. To answer this I shall introduce the concept of a potential prediction (PP for short). Suppose that somewhere along a regularity I make the prediction (h): that it will last at least one-tenth as long again. This prediction is one of the many that could have been made – but usually won't have been – from the beginning to the end, if any, of the continuity, and all of the form: 'This continuity will last at least one-tenth of its previous duration.' Call this class of PPs the *association class of potential predictions* – the APP for short. Then, as a derivation from (T), we have the premiss:

(A) (h) is a member of an APP, at least ten-elevenths of the members of which are true.

So all we need for an inference according to MIP is:

(B) Nothing further is known, rationally believed, or should have been found out about (h)

and we could derive:

(C) It is unreasonable to have other than a high degree of confidence that (h) is true.

Is (B) ever true? It might seem to be true, for we have just said that (h) is *any* prediction of the form required, made during a regularity, and this might sound like an arbitrary prediction of the form required, i.e., one about which nothing more is known. But unfortunately for the first simple version of the argument the crucial point is that *whenever* such a prediction is made something further is known about it, in addition to the fact that it belongs to the APP. It is known that a certain subset of the APP is composed entirely of true predictions, *and (h) is not among them.* For if the regularity *has lasted* t years, those members of the APP made in the first $((10/11) \times t)$ years have already been verified, simply in virtue of the regularity's duration so far. This is in effect Kyburg's point about the next interval not being a random member of the set of intervals.

To make the situation clear, consider an example and an analogy. An example would be this. I suddenly acquire a strange tingle in the knee, a sensation sufficiently unlike any other I know to make evidence from the normal length of occurrence of such sensations untrustworthy. After ten years I wonder whether it is going to continue for another year. Call the prediction that it will (h). Then although (A) and (B) may seem to be true of (h), in fact (B) is false. For another fact is known. It is known that all those PPs which could have been made in the first nine and one-eleventh years of the duration of the tingling are true. For remember that the last one of those, stating that the tingling will last one-tenth as long again, at least, has just been verified as the tingling achieves ten years of life. And it is known that (h) is not among those members of the APP. The difference that this fact makes can be seen if we imagine a parallel. Suppose I know that Johnny attends a school where ten-elevenths of the pupils are little horrors, and I do not know, rationally believe, nor should have found out, anything further about Johnny. Then MIP justifies high confidence that Johnny is a little horror. But suppose I then come to know that some of the children are spoilt, that all of those who are spoilt are little horrors, and that Johnny is not spoilt. How are we to absorb this information? For now all that we know is that Johnny belongs to a class, children at the school who are not spoilt, with a completely unknown little horror proportion: it could be anything from zero, if the spoilt children form ten-elevenths of the school, to nearly ten-elevenths, if the spoilt children form a tiny fraction of the school. There is no particular degree of confidence in Johnny's delinquency which is alone reasonable in this situation, because no particular way of absorbing the information could be shown to have a monopoly of general success. Similarly with (h): we are now in the apparently hopeless position of knowing that it belongs to a sub-class of PPs, those not made in the first nine and one-eleventh years, which could contain any proportion of true PPs from zero, if the tingling stops now, to one if the tingling goes on for ever. But the position may not be quite so hopeless. For while there seems to be no one proper way of redistributing confidence when we learn the further facts about Johnny, it might be shown that certain ways of responding to the realisation that (h) is not in a universally true subset of the PPs would not have a general connection with the truth, and that some other way of responding to this fact is generally right.

The argument revised

Harrod, in effect, tries to establish exactly this.[8] The first point to notice is that one way of restoring the calculation is clearly impossible. In the case of Johnny we could come to know what proportion spoilt children form of the school. We should then have sufficient information to calculate the proportion of little horrors in the remainder, the sub-class to which we know Johnny belongs. Thus if we learn that half the children are spoilt, we know that the other half makes up $(10/11 - \frac{1}{2})$ of the proportion of little horrors, i.e. $9/22$ of them, giving it a little horror proportion of $9/11$. But no analogous piece of information could ever be given in the case of (h). For it would be information of what proportion the nine and one-eleventh years' worth of verified PPs forms of the total APP. But this is equivalent to knowing what proportion of the life of the continuity nine and one-eleventh years represents, i.e. knowing how long the tingling will last. And if we knew this we would know *tout court* whether (h) was true or false. So we can never ask for this piece of information in the inductive case.

Harrod restores his enterprise not by imagining that we can judge what proportion of future PPs, or unverified PPs, are going to be true at any moment, but by instead calculating the arithmetical average of the proportion of future PPs that will be true at all moments. I am afraid this is a bit complicated: it is best understood by means of a diagram (Fig. 4). In this figure AC represents the total number of PPs, n. AB represents those that are true, BC those, coming within one-eleventh of the end, or in general $1/(x + 1)$ of the end, which are false. At any point t in time, as the continuity progresses, ta represents those PPs which are past, and ac those to come, ab represents those to come which are true, and bc those to come which are false. We could also construct a point z, where tz is ten-elevenths of ta, representing those PPs already verified at point a. In terms of the figure the points we have so far made are that at any point, while we know that tb/tc is $10/11$, we also know that (h) does not belong to tz. And we have no way of calculating zb/bc, the success ratio in the smaller class of PPs to which (h) belongs. Furthermore to be given the proportion tz to tc would immediately tell us how far up the continuity we are, and therefore whether (h) is true or false.

[8] Harrod, *Foundations*, pp. 55ff.

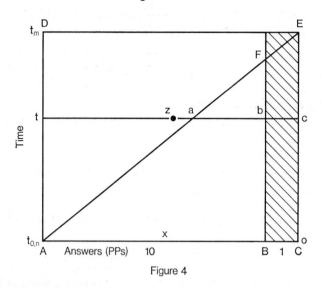

Figure 4

Harrod's restoration is this. He says that although, at any point, we cannot calculate the ratio of true future PPs to total future PPs, what we can calculate is the *average of this ratio,* for all points on the journey. At the beginning the ratio is $10/11$, and at the point F it is zero: the average is the average of the ratio of ab/bc, which is the area AFB to the area AEC, i.e. $10^2/11^2$.

In general when the prediction is that a continuity will continue $1/x$ as long again, the average of the ratio of future true PPs to all future PPs will be $x^2/(x+1)^2$.

Harrod then says that we can take this ratio as the measure of the degree of confidence which it is right to put in any particular prediction. What is the basis of this claim?

Just as the unrevised argument is an attempt to plumb the significance of (T), so this is an attempt to work out the significance of another analyticity:

(T$_2$) If, during the course of a continuity we make the prediction that it will continue at least a tenth as long again as its total duration, then we are following a policy which, followed by any succession of people each starting to make a string of such predictions at regular intervals from beginning to end of the continuity (these people *each* then continuing to make predictions of that form at regular small intervals) gives such a class of predicters an overall success rate of $10^2/11^2$.

Following our previous course, we can attempt to represent the argument as a case of MIP. To bring MIP into play, I shall call the total of all PPs made by the class of predicters described in (T_2) *the aggregate of PPs*. Then:

(A′) (h) is a member of an aggregate of PPs $10^2/11^2$ of which are true,

and

(B′) Nothing further is known, rationally believed or should have been found out about (h).

So:

(C) It is unreasonable to have other than a high degree of confidence that (h) is true.

The difficulty again centres around the premiss (B′). The aggregate described as "all those potential predictions made by all people starting regularly to predict a continuance of at least a tenth as long again, when some start right at the beginning, and others at successive small intervals all the way along the life of the regularity", is indeed an aggregate with the success ratio of $10^2/11^2$. But is nothing else relevant known about (h) than that it is a member of this aggregate?

One thing further is certainly known. It is known – and this is the precise counterpart of the point which rendered revision necessary in the first place – that (h) is not in a completely successful subset of the aggregate of PPs described in (T_2). It is known, that is, that (h) is not in that subset of *verified* PPs, consisting of all the PPs made by potential predicters starting at intervals from the beginning of the tingling, and each regularly predicting until nine and one-eleventh years had passed.

This is the precise counterpart of the point which rendered revision of the argument necessary in the first place. Our prediction, it was said to begin with, is a member of a class of predictions which, necessarily, has a success rate of $10/11$. But, we find, something further, and relevant, is known about it, namely that it is not a member of a completely successful subset. Harrod then offers a way of quantifying the relevance of that comment: we take it into account by saying that in general people starting to make our prediction are right $10^2/11^2$ of the time. That is the success rate of the sum of the strings of predictions made by a set of such people, starting at evenly distributed times throughout the life of the regularity. But then the old point returns that we do know something further about our prediction: it is not in the chunk of the total aggregate which consists of all the regular predictions made by each successive starter from the beginning until nine and one-eleventh years had passed. How relevant is that – does it mean that again any distribution of confidence is equally reasonable, or could we follow the lead set by Harrod's revision of the first version, and try to establish again that it is unreasonable to put much weight on this sort of fact? Is there, in short, a way of showing that general success is *not* to be achieved by letting the existence of the completely successful subsets to which (h) does not belong license any degree of confidence we like in that unfortunate prediction?

A further restatement

It is now fairly clear that whenever we find that we can place an arbitrary prediction (h) in a set with a known high proportion of successes, something further will be known about (h). It will be known that (h) is not in some subset of the set with a 100 per cent success rate, for the existence of such a set is necessary to guarantee the high success rate of the total class or aggregate *whatever happens*. If my analysis is correct this blocks any straightforward reliance on Harrod's arguments. It appears, for all we have said, that some might think this fact about (h) important, and have no confidence in it as a result. Others might let it affect their confidence hardly at all. We have given no way of connecting either of these reactions with general success, so we are not in a position to say that either is uniquely reasonable. But could this be remedied: could a development show that some ways of reacting to this point are exaggeratedly pessimistic and not calculated to give a generally successful policy?

The whole line of thought starts with the fact that over a period of time – when that time includes the start of some continuities – it must happen relatively rarely that we are in the last fraction of the duration of those continuities. The sceptic is not impressed with this; he puts weight on the existence of the duration of the continuity up till now as destroying any guarantee that a predictive policy started *now* will have a high success rate. We then point out, in revising the argument, that even taking this into account, still on the average the policy of predicting at least a one-tenth continuance time has a high success rate. The sceptic replies that this is true if we take the average of people starting to use that policy from beginning to end of the regularity; still, we are not at the beginning of the regularity, we are, in my example, ten years through its life, so averages of success rates from beginning to end of the continuity do not interest him.

But we in turn can wonder how little interest a sceptic could be entitled to betray in such an average. Let us consider a Humean sceptic,[9] one who thinks that any degree of confidence in the one-tenth continuance is as justified as any other. An instance of the claim is then that a degree of confidence of $\frac{1}{4}$ – that appropriate to a card taken at random from a shuffled pack being a spade – is as justified as $10^2/11^2$. This degree of confidence, $\frac{1}{4}$, is that held by someone who is prepared to bet at three to one against the one-tenth continuance, i.e. he is reasonably confident that the regularity will stop. This is as justifiable as that degree of confidence that it will not finish, according to the Humean sceptic. We try to attack this claim by pointing out that $\frac{1}{4}$ is the degree of confidence appropriate to use of a policy which goes wrong three times out of four; but, we say, it is a very rare event indeed for someone to start predicting a one-tenth continuance somewhere along a regularity, and be wrong three times out of four. The inevitable reply is that this is a rare event only in the class of possible users of that policy from beginning to end of the regularity, and we are not at the beginning, we are ten years through it. Yes, but what connection with success enables a pessimist to use *that* fact to justify, at least as far as any other prediction, the expectation that the regularity will finish?

The possibility that comes to light is that we can twist the subject of a use of MIP to *a particular case of using a certain argument*. The idea is that the Humean sceptic's defence of confidence of $\frac{1}{4}$ is an instance of a use of an argument which itself gives the wrong answer most of the time. The full statement of this idea is as follows:

(A″) At most points t during a continuity, if someone started to consider a one-tenth continuance, and used the fact that the life of t years was already gone to justify high confidence that the continuance would not come about, his prediction would be wrong.

[9] See pp. 42–4.

(B″) Nothing further is known, rationally believed, or should have been discovered to show that the present instant is uncharacteristic in this respect.

So:

(C″) At the present instant it is reasonable to expect such a prediction of change, justified solely as indicated, to be wrong.

This appears to me to be altogether more formidable than the first two versions of the argument. We have taken someone who, following the sceptic's liberality, believes prediction of change to be as justifiable as prediction of continuance. When we confront him with the high average success rate of a policy of expecting continuance, he replies by citing a certain fact. What we have now done is argued that in general use of that fact to justify prediction of a change leads to failure, so that unless something special is known about its use on this occasion, it is unreasonable to believe a prediction justified solely through reliance on it.

Is (B″) generally true? It need not be true, of course. It could easily be known, to take again the example of the tingling, that many similar continuous sensations cease after ten years. Alternatively since the prediction is being made at a certain time (e.g. 21 June 1972), there may be reason to believe that such continuities will end at that time, perhaps because a rather large bomb is going to be dropped. But we are not considering the situation where we have collateral information of this sort, we are considering what it is rational to expect in its absence. And in its absence, what could be generally true which would make (B″) false? The relevant respect is that it should be more likely that the use of a certain argument at the present instant is going to lead to success than it usually is. To defeat this use of MIP, therefore, the sceptic must show that when we are some arbitrary time through the duration of a regularity there will be more reason to place weight on the fact that we are an arbitrary time through the regularity than would appear justified by the (rather low) success rate generally obtained by placing weight on this fact. And I confess that I can see no prospect of his doing this.

In short, suppose that we are told this of a sceptic. We are told that he knew that a regularity had lasted ten years, and used this fact to justify not taking the average success of one-tenth continuance predictions as relevant; but counted the contrary prediction as grounded just as well or badly. Then using only MIP we can say that since in general use of this form of argument leads to the view that false predictions are as justifiable as true ones, and nothing further is known about this case, no weight should be attached to the sceptic's manoeuvre in this particular case.

Further possibilities

The whole line of the argument might be summed up aphoristically by saying that the exception cannot be the rule; therefore it is generally wrong to take it to be going to start being the rule in the near future. And if this is generally wrong, then, without special reason, it is wrong now. Faced with the failure of the first two versions of the argument, the vital twist is to take as the subject for a use of MIP not the predominantly successful classes to which (h) belongs, but rather the predominantly unsuccessful classes of argument to which the sceptic's move of emphasising the weight of a certain fact belongs.

Nothing in the argument guarantees future success, even of the limited, fractional continuance predictions we have considered. Anything might happen; but then, as we have seen, the problem is not to guarantee our experience following some uniform course, but to guarantee the rationality of expecting it to do so. If the argument of this chapter is correct it is no good to repeat that anything might happen, for we simply reply that even if this is true, still the end of a continuity is a relatively rare event, and our principles can be brought to bear to forbid confidence in its imminent occurrence.

It is necessary to say a little about how comprehensive this argument is. Its application is not entirely restricted to cases where, apart from our knowledge that a regularity has continued for a certain time, we are entirely ignorant. Suppose, in a certain case, we had collateral information about the duration of previous similar regularities. In the tingling case, we might have learned that previous sufferers generally found that the sensation died away after ten years. This might be good news: I might take their experience as a guide to what mine will be like, and so take (h) to be false. I expect one regularity (the continuance of the sensation) to cease, because I expect another regularity (such sensations lasting ten years) to continue to cover my case. I mightn't do this, because I might reasonably think that I am different from others – perhaps I know that my headaches and so forth tend to persist longer. But if the phenomenon of the sensation ceasing after ten years has been well established, then it will be a reasonable thing to do to expect it to cover my case. Otherwise we are expecting, arbitrarily, a particular instance to be the first break in *that* regularity, and the argument of this chapter can be brought into play to condemn us.

It will be common to find conflicting regularities, i.e., cases in which the continuance of one would lead to one thing, the continuance of the other to a different thing. The argument of this chapter does not, of course, command us to place confidence in the extrapolation of each of two regularities, when they conflict. When two conflicting but well-founded regularities come to our notice, then something further is known about the prediction that either will continue: namely that its truth involves the other breaking. This is just as it is: part of the process of empirical investigation is one of finding which similarities tend to survive such clashes, and so which analogies and regularities enable us to see sudden change as a part of continuing order. When we have done such empirical work, we can give the palm of confidence to whichever phenomenon has had the greater scope, and has been seen over a greater time or in the greater number of instances. The justification of extrapolation that I have offered naturally encourages this procedure, for the greater the range of a regularity, the smaller the extrapolation we are making in expecting it to cover a further instance, and the greater the confidence that we can afford ourselves.

Another vexed issue in the philosophy of science which we can now allow ourselves to say something about is the problem of suppositious instances of something. This is often unfortunately described as the problem of counterfactual conditionals, but it is the same problem whenever we try to reason from the supposition that something is, will be, or was, the case, whether or not we also think this supposition contrary to fact. "If the burglar had come through here, he would have left a trace" may be said whether or not we expect to find that the burglar did come through here. We may use it if we expect to argue that because he went through here, there must be a trace, or if we expect to argue that because there is no trace, he didn't go through here. It is rational to make such a claim if it is rational to suppose that a certain regularity can be taken to cover the supposed case. Notoriously, it is often unclear just what is being supposed, and this confuses the issue. Often the only reply to an assertion like "If Hitler had invaded Britain, he would have reached London" will be that we must spell out the supposition in much more detail – are we imagining him to have invaded without air cover and so forth?

When the supposition is described in reasonable detail (and the amount will vary from subjects where details matter more, like history, to subjects where they matter less, like physics) it may become reasonable to extend some regularity to cover it. The important thing is that the rationality of taking a regularity to cover a supposed instance is no different from the rationality of expecting it to cover any further, unobserved instance. The man who reasonably expects the sun to rise at seven o'clock is the man who can reasonably say, when he wakes in the dark, that if it were after seven o'clock the sun would have risen. The doctor who reasonably thinks that the next fracture he comes across will be painful to the patient reasonably thinks that if this were a fracture it would be painful. The connection of reasoning with success assures us of this directly, for the man who is generally successful in his expectations is also generally successful in arguing by extending his basis for expectation to cover argument about suppositious instances. That is, if we are generally correct in expecting fractures to be painful, we are also generally correct in arguing that if something were a fracture it would be painful, and either concluding that it is painful or that it's not a fracture. A justification for expectation is therefore a justification for belief in subjunctive conditionals, and although I haven't said anything about general laws, with which, obscurely, they are usually discussed, we need worry no further about them.

It may be that the argument of this chapter exhausts the scope of a direct approach to the problem. By this I mean that further advance may have to enrich the rather sparse conceptual landscape which we have drawn for our predictor. He may possess concepts – he may need to possess them if he thinks at all – which themselves have some connection with the rationality of his procedures. A sceptic may then try to say that the indefensibility of induction just shows that use of those concepts is unjustifiable, but this may not be an easy claim to support. The most general concept which appears fundamental to our way of thinking, and perhaps to any way of thinking, is that of an object of an external world. This is a concept which certainly seems to have some connection with the existence of regularities and resemblances in experience, and we now turn to the question of whether this connection can be put to the purpose of defending inductive reasoning.

8

Objectivity and prediction

Expectations

Is the ordinary man good at predicting? If this question were
whether the ordinary man is good at stating predictions which turn
out to be true, the answer would depend on the ordinary man.
Perhaps some ordinary men only bother to state predictions about
interesting but chancy matters, like horse races or the weather, and
very likely most of their stated predictions would then be false.
But they presumably hold other expectations, and the possibility
arises that their success rate in general is very different from that
obtaining amongst those expectations which they formulate as predictions.[1] Now if some of these expectations which we hold but do
not state are inductively based, it is not at all easy to see how we
could estimate the past success of the relevant policy. For example,
If I pick up a piece of paper to type upon I certainly expect it not
to explode. Is this then one case of successful use of an inductive
policy (most pieces of paper in a wide variety of circumstances have
failed to explode when picked up; so probably this one will not
explode)? If so, then there are countless successful cases of using
such policies throughout our lives.

On the other hand, if we refuse to admit such an expectation to
within the province of the problem of induction, so much the
worse for our conception of the problem of induction. For such an

[1] Ignoring this distinction obscures much of Shoemaker's discussion of
the truth of *most* memory claims (*Self-Knowledge and Self-Identity*, 1963,
pp. 229–36). Shoemaker has one argument that most of a man's stated
memory claims must be true (otherwise we can't be sure that he uses
words like "remember" correctly: this is a bad argument because
memory claims are frequently made without using any such word, and
we can use such a word without making memory claims); and another
argument that most memory beliefs must be true. He then identifies the
two conclusions: '...one's own sincere and confident perceptual and
memory statements, i.e., one's own confident perceptual and memory
beliefs...' (p. 233). But nobody is or could be that voluble.

expectation as that about the piece of paper, or my expectation that my typewriter will remain black, is eminently reasonable as well as immensely common, so to consider only *stated* expectations is to arbitrarily restrict the problem. It is this restriction which enables some writers, such as Black and Braithwaite,[2] to think of determining the past success rate of any inductive policy as a straightforward historical investigation. For it is theoretically possible to count the number of predictions stated and stated to be based in a certain way, but not so clearly theoretically possible to count the number of expectations held for a certain reason.

What criterion can be used for possessing an expectation which is not stated? Preparedness to bet is one which lends itself to quantitative treatment. But it involves certain idealisations, and a simpler suggestion for our purposes is:

(E) At t_0 X expects P (where P is a proposition stating that something will be true at or throughout some future time) if and only if X would be surprised at $\sim$ P upon coming to know it at t_0.

There are a small number of remarks to be made about (E). A man might expect P at t_0 but not be surprised when P is falsified later, because he might have changed his mind in the interval, or, more mundanely, because he didn't know that P had been falsified. So we take account of these by stipulating that it is upon coming to know of its falsity, at the time at which he is said to hold the expectation, that the man is surprised. Furthermore it must be $\sim$ P that X is surprised *at*. I might be surprised upon coming to know some State Secret, not because I had expected the negation of the secret, but simply because I had expected never to know any State Secrets. The condition simply that X is surprised upon coming to know $\sim$ P doesn't specify what it is in the situation that X is surprised *at*, and thus fails by itself to capture the intensionality in the 'X expects P'.

(E) provides an extremely liberal criterion for possessing an expectation: we expect, according to it, many things which we have never consciously considered. For example, I expect, according to (E), something to be true in the near future of each of the objects in my room: I expect them not to blow up, change colour, disappear,

[2] Black, "The Inductive Support of Inductive Rules", *Problems of Analysis*, 1954, ch. XI; Braithwaite, *Scientific Explanation*, 1960, ch. VIII.

suddenly become immensely heavy, fly around and so on; for any of them doing such a thing would surprise me, even although I have never consciously considered, far less talked about, the possibility of them behaving so. Furthermore there is no doubt that as we have moved about the objects of the external world such expectations have been continuously verified, and particular possible surprises have failed to occur.

The most obvious expectations which we possess concern the future *existence*, *whereabouts*, and *properties* of the objects of our acquaintance, for these expectations pre-eminently guide our everyday movements and planning. Are such expectations inductively-based? It seems obvious that many are. The simplest class is that of expectations concerning the future possession of a property by an object. For here it is often an essential part of our reason for such a belief that the object has had that property in the past. Of course there may be other propositions supporting our confidence in our expectation as well, but let us just consider the way in which belief that an object has had a property forms an essential part of our reason of expecting it to have it. A way of characterising this condition is that the following are jointly true:

(1) The person expects object o to be φ at or throughout some time.
(2) The person believes that object o has been φ.
(3) If the person ceased to believe that o had been φ, he would cease to expect it to be φ.[3]

These three together give a sufficient condition for a person's expectation that an object will have a property to be based upon the evidence that it has had it, in the sense that the evidence forms an essential part of the person's reason for his expectation. Again, for these three to be satisfied the person does not have to have consciously considered the conclusion, the reason for it, nor to have

[3] Note that this condition is not: 'If the person hadn't believed that o was φ he would not expect it to be φ", which refers to the genesis of a belief, not its basis. It is easy to think of cases where this counterfactual is true (say because if the person hadn't believed that o was φ he would not have gone to an oracle which he trusts, and which informed him that o would continue to be φ), but where the knowledge of the past is not an essential part of the man's reason for his expectation, precisely because (3) is false.

reasoned from one to the other. And again, the justification for considering such expectations is that we hold an immense number of them, they are often reasonable, and it would be part of the purpose of a Humean sceptic about induction to deny that they are uniquely reasonable, i.e., to deny that it is uniquely right or justifiable to vary one's expectations with one's knowledge of the past, in the way described in (3).

The question I want to ask now is whether, in the course of experience of a world of external objects, most such expectations could be false. Can we imagine a course of experience which is experience of a world of physical objects, in which we possess such expectations, based on the past possession of properties by the objects of that world, but in which most such expectations are falsified during that course of experience? There are a number of expressions which need clarification if we are properly to grasp this question.

The first is the idea of *most* inductively-based expectations of the sort described. With the criterion (E) can we count our expectations? Clearly, a person has as many expectations about objects as there are propositions of the form 'o will be φ' which satisfy the subjunctive conditional in (E), and as many that are inductively based as satisfy (2) and (3) as well.

But now consider my inductively based expectation that my typewriter will continue to be black for half an hour. This expectation entails a host of others: my typewriter will be black for five minutes, for the next thirty seconds, for the period of five minutes commencing in twenty-five minutes' time: it will not be red in ten minutes, not be green in ten minutes, and so on. Each of these propositions is different, and each satisfies the criteria for an inductively based expectation of an object. But then we possess an unlimited medley of expectations, entailed by any expectation which we hold: how can we count them, as a step to giving criteria for *most* having some property?[4] It seems to me that, literally, we cannot count them. Nevertheless we can, I think, give an acceptable reconstruction of the idea of most of them being true.

Consider firstly the problem raised by time. If I expect an object o to be φ for the next half an hour, this entails that I expect it to be φ for any period we care to describe within that half-hour. If the object suddenly ceased to be φ at some time within that half-hour, when are we to say that most such expectations are falsified? The

---

[4] The same problem arises with the notion of most beliefs of any kind.

simplest answer is that we say that most are falsified if the object is $\sim\varphi$ for most of the period, and most are true if the object is φ for most of the period. Remembering that our ultimate purpose is to characterise the *success* of a fairly weak policy of expectation, we should accept this criterion in spite of its artificiality, for we are generally successful if objects possess the properties we expect for most of the time for which we expect them to possess them.

Then there is the problem of properties possession of which is entailed by other inductively based expectations. If I expect my typewriter to be black, I expect it to be not-yellow, not-red, not-blue, not-pink, etc. Also, these each count as inductively based, by (2) and (3). For I believe my typewriter not to have been yellow, and if I ceased to believe this, e.g., because someone shows me that the black is just dirt covering the original yellow colour, I will expect it to continue yellow. But if we allow these expectations as counting in favour of a policy, we make the problem too easy for ourselves and its solution irrelevant to the problem of justification. For most of these expectations *must* be true, simply because at any time a typewriter can only be (predominantly) one colour. So most of the beliefs of the form 'it will be not-yellow, not-red, not-blue, etc.' must be true, since only one can be false. But although this provides a class of expectations which because of their logical relations cannot be mostly false, it does nothing to reflect confidence on the expectation that the typewriter will be black. For if most of the members of the class: 'it will be black, not-red, not-yellow, not-green. . .' must be true, so equally must most members of the class: 'it will be green, not-black, not-yellow, not-red. . .'. All we really have here is a slightly different form of the point made in chapter 4, that most differentiating hypotheses: 'it will become yellow, it will become red. . .' must be false because of their mutual inconsistency;[5] we now reap the consequence that most expectations of their falsity must be true. But this does nothing to justify the expectation that the typewriter will be black, as against expectation that it will be green: both, it seems, are members of a class of predictions 'it will be C where C is some specific colour' most of which are false; both are members of another class 'it will be C and not-A, not-B. . .where A, B. . .are other colours' most of which must be true. But then we have failed to distinguish them in point of rationality.

[5] See above, p. 94.

To eliminate this feature of the success of everyday expectations I suggest we restrict attention to what I shall call *primary* expectations. It is true that my belief that my typewriter will not be yellow satisfies (2) and (3). It is also true that I believe that my typewriter will not be yellow because I expect it to stay black, i.e., because I have, on inductive grounds, some other specific colour in mind for it. It is quite clear that there is a one-way relationship here: it would be natural to reply to someone who asked why I expect it not to be yellow, that it is because I expect it to be black, but not to say that I expect it to be black because I expect it to be not-yellow, not-red, etc. I suggest then that where there are a number of exclusive alternatives under some concept, and I expect a thing to satisfy one of them, the expectations that it will not satisfy any of the others, which I hold in consequence, should be considered secondary, and not taken into account in assessing the success rate of a policy of expectation.

The perception of change

We are now in a good position to answer the question with which I began the chapter. The ordinary man, it seems, is extremely good at predicting. For we all spend most of our lives *not* being surprised, because primary inductively based expectations turn out to be true, when their not doing so would most certainly have surprised us. The further question is, granted that this is so, can we imagine what it would be like for it not to be so? What degree of chaos could have the result that we are surprised at the failure of primary inductively based expectations about the properties of objects, literally more often than not?[6]

We are not, of course, asking whether most of a person's primary inductively based expectations might not break down *now*. It is quite possible, logically, that all objects should cease to exist now, or that most of them should, or that most or all objects should suddenly change in some drastic way in most respects. A sudden catastrophe with such consequences is possible, no doubt, but it is the idea of continuous chaos that we are to concentrate upon. It is however instructive to notice one feature of the sudden cataclysm

[6] The thought here is perhaps similiar to that expressed in Wittgenstein, *Tractatus Logico-Philosophicus*, 1961, 6. 362: "What can be described can also happen: and what the law of causality is meant to exclude cannot even be described."

which falsifies most expectations, and this is that nobody could have good evidence that it had occurred. Suppose, for example, that my experience continues throughout the dislocation. Am I to think that I am continuing to perceive the external world, and that it is undergoing this cataclysmic change? There is the at least equally plausible view that something has gone wrong with me and my perceptual apparatus; that the apparent disappearance and meta-morphosis of familiar objects is not real, but that they remain and my perceptions of them have failed. Nor is the testimony of other people any help, for the public verifiability of the existence of a cataclysm is only any help if I can locate a public whom I believe to have been in the same position, and to whom I can appeal for confirmation of what I apparently saw. But if most of my inductively based expecta-tions about other people failed too, this cannot be done.

It appears then that we can imagine at least two, and possibly three, different views which I could hold to account for a sufficiently drastic discontinuity of experience. I could think that the world of familiar objects had suddenly changed, and that most of my induc-tively based expectations had been falsified; or I could think that something awful had happened to my perceptual apparatus, but there was no good reason to suppose that the world had altered; thirdly, I could perhaps come to the conclusion that I had been transported to a different part of space, or a different space, and was now perceiving a different set of things altogether. Again, there would be no good reason for supposing that most of my inductively based expectations had been falsified; it is just that I am no longer in a position to tell.

Because of the rival hypotheses it appears that I can never be in a position to know that most of my inductively based expectations about the continued properties of objects and people have suddenly been falsified. However nasty experience turned out to be, I could never be assured that it was a course of experience of an external world which was just changing in a thoroughgoing way. However, we must not overestimate the importance of this result. For it would be unduly verificationist to conclude that no meaning can be attached to the hypothesis of a change which falsifies most primary induc-tively based expectations about objects. It would also be unduly veri-ficationist to conclude that the three hypotheses are logically equi-valent, although this is an identification which will appeal to a phenomenalistic philosophy of perception. That is, if we think that my experience having a certain regularity is *what it is* for me to be perceiving an external world, then such experiences lapsing into sudden disorder is *what it is* for me to be perceiving an external world which suddenly changes drastically. This view would then identify the different hypotheses which account for the discontinuity; yet this does not seem right.[7] For after the discontinuity I might surely wonder whether things have really altered as they seemed to me to do, and this wonderment might make a good deal of difference to my state of mind, even although there is nothing I can do to settle my doubt.

In any case, there is some difficulty in being assured of a sudden falsification of most primary inductive expectations about the future properties and existence of objects. But if this is so for a *sudden* change falsifying beliefs about the immediate future, it is much more so for a continuous change or succession of changes, falsifying beliefs about the immediate future all the time, or most of the time. Yet it is this that we want to consider. For if a sudden drastic change happened, although it would falsify most primary inductive expectations which I hold now, it would not follow that induction had been an unsuccessful policy for me to follow throughout the whole course of my experience, for previous to this my success in expectation has been remarkable. What we are trying to consider is a course of experience where this is not so; where there is not merely a failure of expectations at one point, but where there is no general success at all throughout the preceding course. The feeling that one has, contemplating this, is that such experience could not be rationally considered to be experience of a world of independent external objects.

Part of the unclarity in this investigation is due to our failure to describe more carefully the strength of the policies we are considering. For example, suppose someone is tremendously conservative, and whenever an object in his ken has possessed a property for ten

[7] This is one interpretation of the view of Bennett, *Kant's Analytic*, 1966, §§ 11–13. This passage, and also Strawson, *Individuals*, 1959, ch. 2 ("Sounds"), are extremely helpful in connecting regularity in experience with the distinction between what is and what seems to be the case, and hence with perception of an external world. But there is room for clarity on whether regular experience is a necessary condition of the seems/is distinction being (i) rationally employed, (ii) truly employed, or whether it is supposed to be a sufficient condition of the last, which is the view discussed above.

seconds, he is confident that it will stay the same for ten years. Surely we can imagine most of his expectations being falsified, for by our criterion this would be true if the object changed after any time less than five years, and it is not at all difficult to imagine a world in which most objects change most properties within such a time. The point is, in Bennett's useful phrase, that there has to be a "speed limit" if perception is reasonably supposed to be of an external but changing world. Inductive policies which this approach can hope to justify must not then be so ambitious that they could be generally unsuccessful even if the "speed limit" is observed.

The strategy of the argument then is that the objects with which we are acquainted must possess some stability – continue to exist, stay in the same place, possess the same properties – if we are to suppose rationally that we are perceiving an external world at all, and that this stability is sufficient to guarantee the truth of most expectations formed, over a period of time, in accordance with a sufficiently unambitious predictive policy. How are we to translate this into the rationality of particular primary inductively based expectations which we hold *now*? After all, the external world might cease to exist now: what use is it then to be told that *if* we are to take ourselves to continue to perceive it, most inductively based expectations must be true?

There are two answers to this challenge. The first depends upon the apparatus discussed in the previous two chapters, which enables us to develop the argument as follows:

(1) It is rational to suppose that we are perceiving and have been perceiving an external world, of independently existing objects.

(2) This can only be so if experience is extremely stable in respect of perceived change, disappearance, motion, of such objects.

(3) This stability ensures the general success of a sufficiently weak inductive policy (call it I) over the period of existence of such a world.

(4) That is, at most moments in the existence of such a world, most expectations sanctioned by I will be true.

(5) By (1) it is rational to believe that the present moment is one at which such a world exists.

(6) Nothing is known, rationally believed, or should have been discovered to indicate that the present moment is unusual in the respect mentioned in (4).

(7) Therefore, by MIP, it is rational to suppose that most expectations sanctioned by I, and now held, will be true.

The similarity of this argument to the revised version of Harrod's argument, propounded in the previous chapter, lies simply in the move of finding a proposition stating that something is true at most times, and using MIP to derive the irrationality of supposing that it is false now. It would be pleasant to be able to describe more fully the degree of stability of the world, and hence the strength of policy I, which the regularity in experience which is necessary for objectivity can guarantee, but I see no straightforward prospect of doing this. Indeed, I doubt very much whether quantitative precision is possible or desirable here. For there is no obvious measure of the degree of regularity which a course of experience would have to possess for it to be rationally considered experience of independent objects; nor do our actual predictive policies give quantitatively precise measures of the appropriate confidence in many expectations.

We saw in the preceding chapters that the issues surrounding the move from premisses like (5) and (6) to conclusions such as (7) are complicated, although I have argued that MIP must be accepted. But it is interesting that we can provide another route from (1), (2) and (3), to a conclusion about rational prediction, a route which throws new light on the connection between regularity and objectivity.

Further connections

Suppose we succeed in demonstrating that in the course of a world of independent objects, most primary inductively based expectations concerning their properties, formed according to some suitably weak policy I, must be true. We can imagine a sceptic about induction replying that this only shows that *if* it is rational to expect a world of objects to continue to a certain time, *then* it is rational to expect most such expectations relating to that time to be true. But if we eschew the argument above we have done nothing to demonstrate the truth of the antecedent, that it is rational to expect the world of independent objects to continue to exist for any time at all.

Let us concentrate then upon the future existence of the objects of the external world. There is no question but that we all possess expectations that objects with which we are acquainted will continue to exist for at least limited periods of time, and of course many of these expectations are entailed by others, namely that the objects will have certain properties at certain times. Now the philosophical logic of these expectations is interesting, and possesses one feature in particular which bears on the problem of their justification. Consider the expectation I possess of an object, which I would express by pointing at the object or otherwise indicating it, and saying: "This will exist in ten minutes' time." This is a prediction: what is the inductive evidence for it? Partly of course there is indirect evidence from the longevity of other similar objects. But also there is knowledge of the object's present and past existence. But we get a very curious situation if we ask whether this knowledge is a reason for the prediction. For our analysis of the concept of a reason demands that to tell whether one proposition is a reason for another it must be possible to have confidence in the conclusion before, and after, coming to know the premiss: the question is then whether this confidence ought to be increased upon the acquisition of this knowledge.[8] Now this comparison of confidence in the conclusion before and after coming to know the evidence demands that it should be possible to *understand* the conclusion before coming to know the evidence: otherwise it will be impossible to have any degree of confidence whatsoever in the conclusion, before knowing the evidence. Yet it is just this condition which is not satisfied in the case where the conclusion is: 'This object will exist in ten minutes' time' (said pointing out some object) and the evidence is: 'This object exists now and has existed in the past.' For to understand this conclusion it must be known *which* object is being indicated, and knowing which object is being indicated entails knowing of its present existence. It is true that if I heard anyone utter the sentence "This object will exist in ten minutes" when I was not in a position to see which object he was talking about, I would not find his utterance unintelligible, but equally, not knowing what he was talking about, I would not know *which prediction he was making*. Not knowing which prediction he is making, there is no prediction in which I can have such-and-such a degree of confidence; therefore, no prediction in which my confidence can be, or ought to be, increased, when I learn of the identity, and therefore of the present existence, of the object to which the speaker referred.

This clearly complicates enormously any attempt at a direct discussion of whether the present existence of objects is a reason, or

[8] See above, p. 23.

part of the reason, for expectation of their future existence. Indeed, it seems to me that it blocks such a direct approach completely, leaving no possibility of comparison of justified confidence before and after coming to know what is not only the evidence, but also a precondition of identifying the prediction. Fortunately we can discuss directly the rationality of the prediction of future existence, without discussing directly its relation to the inductive evidence, simply by considering the truth of most such predictions.

The sceptic we are to consider is drawing the teeth of the connection between objectivity and regularity, by claiming that it is wrong[9] to have a high degree of confidence that the external world will continue to exist for any time into the future. Now if it is wrong to have confidence in this, then, taking any arbitrary object in the external world, it is wrong to have confidence that that will exist in the future. For we can't have more confidence that an object in the external world will exist than we have that the external world will exist. So if we consider a particular thing, say the Albert Memorial, this sceptic is asserting that it is wrong to have a high degree of confidence that this will exist in the future, and similarly for any object we care to name.

On the other hand this sceptic is prepared to admit that we are right to have confidence that the external world exists now. We are not considering a man who is sceptical about perception, and hence about the evidence on which we base inductive expectations: this is a sceptic about the predictions made on that evidence. Now if we are right to have confidence that the external world exists, we are right to have confidence that many objects in the world exist *at present unperceived* by us. For this is essentially involved in belief in a world of independently existing external objects: to hold that belief is to hold that there are continuous objects, amongst which we move, and which exist whether or not we are at the moment perceiving them. This belief the sceptic grants. So there are objects, he allows, which I cannot at the moment perceive, but which I am justified in supposing to exist at present. Let us suppose that the Albert Memorial is one of these. Then:

(R) It is right for me to have confidence that the Albert Memorial exists now, unperceived by me.

[9] I consider firstly this strong version of scepticism (see p. 42) just for the sake of simplicity in the statement of the argument.

(N) It is wrong for me to have confidence that the Albert Memorial will exist in the future – at any future time.

This scepticism is a general position, about what our attitude to the future ought always to be. So as a concomitant to (N), we have:

(F) Fifteen minutes ago it would have been wrong for me to have had confidence that the Albert Memorial would exist in fifteen minutes' time (i.e. now).

The question of course is: in virtue of what wasn't it reasonable to suppose fifteen minutes ago that the Albert Memorial would exist now, whereas it is reasonable now to suppose that it exists now? We were, apparently, wrong to have confidence that a state of affairs would exist, but right now to have confidence that it does exist. Nor need we imagine any direct evidence coming to light in the interval: in general there are many objects which I do not perceive such that I (wrongly, according to this scepticism) have confidence that they will exist, and also at a later time (rightly, according to this scepticism) have confidence that they do exist, without receiving any evidence specifically relating to them in the interval.

Again, it is worth while emphasising the universal existence of these beliefs. We are all continually ceasing to look at certain objects, expecting them to be there in a short time, and believing throughout that time that they exist at the present moment. It is over the continually recurring situation, of holding a belief that a state of affairs now exists where it was formerly expected that it would not exist, that this scepticism is in difficulty. Clearly, the first thing for the sceptic to attempt is to reconcile (R) and (F). Asked why it was wrong to expect something which it is now right to suppose is the case, the form of the answer must be that some knowledge or rational belief has come to light in the interval to justify raised confidence. Thus, to take the example, if I now think that the Albert Memorial exists (now), but didn't previously think that it would exist now, I must justify myself by citing some evidence that has come to light in the interval. In general, the only type of evidence I come to know, over an interval in which I do not learn anything about an absent physical object, is that the objects in my immediate environment have continued to exist over the interval. So we can imagine the sceptic saying that (F) is true, because he is sceptical about predictions of future existence; (R) is true, because it is rational to believe in the existence of the external world; and the increase in confidence in the Albert Memorial existing now is accounted for by my knowledge, obtained in the interval, that other objects have continued to exist until now.

It may help to present the general form of the argument. The charge is that a sceptic about predictions of existence who is not a sceptic about the external world, believes for some unperceived objects o, the following three things:

(i) It is right to have confidence at t_0 that o exists at t_0.
(ii) It is not right to have confidence at t_0 that o will exist at t_1.
(iii) It is right to have confidence at t_1 that o exists at t_1.

(ii) and (iii) describe an allegedly rational increase in confidence in a proposition. We ask in virtue of what this is rational, and the only answer can be: because of some knowledge obtained in the interval. But all we need suppose obtained in the interval is the knowledge (K) that some other objects than o have existed until t_1 But to use (K) to justify increasing confidence in the existence at t_1 of o is to *use an inductive argument*. If I justify believing that the Albert Memorial exists now, whereas I didn't believe that it would fifteen minutes ago, on the grounds that some objects with which I am acquainted still exist, I am using their stability over the interval to justify the supposition that the Albert Memorial has existed over the interval, and this is an inductive argument.

The important principle is this. We can force the sceptic to a position where he has to justify having a different degree of confidence in a proposition at different times. This proposition can be one for which no direct evidence was discovered in the interval. Only one sort of fact need have been discovered in the interval. The sceptic must then say that it is this fact which justifies the increase of confidence. But to use this fact to justify an increase in confidence is to use an inductive argument: it is to say that because objects in my ken have continued to exist, so have others. The argument then concludes that the sceptic must either admit the rationality of certain predictions of existence, or use an inductive argument from the existence of observed objects to that of unobserved ones.

Furthermore, the inductive argument from (K) which is to justify the joint holding of (ii) and (iii) need not be very strong. For I might not know that many objects have continued to exist in the interval. I may for example have been asleep in the interval; I wake up knowing that my bed and body and one or two other objects still exist, but if, as the sceptic claims, it was wrong of me to have confidence that all the other objects of which I know would exist when I woke up, then it would be a strikingly weak inductive argument to derive assurance that they all do just from the fact that I and my bed do. In other words, if we consider a case where (ii) really is true, where it really is wrong of me to be confident that a certain object will exist at a certain time, then it is not at all clear that it would be a very strong argument to use (K) to allay this doubt when the time has arrived. But if it is doubtful whether the inductive argument from (K) will do the work the sceptic requires of it – and employing it he is in any case being an inductivist – then he is left with no alternative but to abandon the joint assertion of (ii) and (iii). He must either forfeit his scepticism about induction, or his belief in the external world.

It is surprising that such a strong argument should exist, and each step and the significance of the conclusion must therefore be given the greatest scrutiny.

Must the sceptic accept (i) and (iii)? The answer is that he must, for he believes in the existence of the external world, and this entails believing in the existence of objects unperceived by him. Must he accept (ii)? Apparently, for this merely states his scepticism, saying that at any time it is wrong to have confidence that objects will exist at future times. But this is a strong form of scepticism, and I shall briefly discuss two modifications.

Firstly the Humean sceptic would say that he doesn't claim that it is wrong to have confidence in the prediction of future existence, only that it is *equally right* to be doubtful about it. (ii) would then have to be reformed to state that it is not wrong not to believe at t_0 that o will exist at t_1. But this liberalism doesn't affect the argument, for the rationality of belief in the external world entails that it *is* wrong not to have confidence at t_1 that o exists at t_1, so still there is a change in status of the belief, and it is this change that the sceptic is being called upon to justify. Secondly a sceptic might say that he doesn't wish to claim that *at any time* it is wrong to make these predictions, only that it is irrational *now*. Five minutes ago it was rational to expect the Albert Memorial to exist now, just as it is rational now to suppose that it exists now, but it is not rational *now* to suppose that it will exist in five minutes' time. But if scepticism ceases to be a general position about what our attitude to the future ought to be it ceases to be very interesting. A person who says that generally it is reasonable to make these predictions, but not now, who therefore holds (N) but not (F) in terms of our original example, should give some account of this singularity of the present moment: to say what the difference between the present and the near past is, such that predictions were rational then but are not now.

If (i), (ii) and (iii) are secure, we then ask how the sceptic proposes to justify his distinct difference in confidence. Is it true that he can only use the inductive argument based on (K)? Of course, there are cases where I learn something specifically relating to the object o between t_0 and t_1. I may doubt whether the Albert Memorial will exist in ten minutes because I have placed a bomb under it, and learn after five minutes that I have forgotten the detonator, and so have confidence at the end of the interval that it still exists. But such cases are, to say the least, relatively rare, and it is the general belief in unperceived existence which is a consequence of belief in the external world. And what in general could we have to go on except (K), the knowledge that those objects which we can directly perceive, have lasted over the interval t_0 to t_1?

Conclusion

Suppose that someone accepted all this, but was inclined to reverse the argument. Granted, he might say, that the rationality of belief in the external world entails the rationality of belief in certain predictions of existence, might not *that* just be used to show that the irrationality of belief in those predictions entails the irrationality of belief in the external world? Objectivity, it might be said, is not a firm enough anchor for expectations of regularity. There are two answers to this. The first is that we are considering the relation between what is observed and remembered and what is expected. What is observed and remembered is described in objective terms: it is observed and remembered that my chair is green, heavy, a member of a class of things which tend to exist for long periods, and so on. It is the rationality of the prediction that the chair will exist in ten minutes that we consider, taking ourselves to know that it is a chair, exists as an object in the external world, and has certain properties. Now of course it is open to a sceptic to deny that we know this (which is not to say that it would be right for him to do so) but this entirely changes the character of his scepticism. He is no longer denying the right to make certain predictions upon certain evidence, but denying that we ever know the evidence. But it is to the former problem that this enquiry is directed, and whatever success it achieves is not diminished by raising the latter. Secondly, and more fundamentally, it is not so easy to claim that we do not know that there exist objective particulars, or that it is wrong to be confident that they exist. For there exists argument that objective, re-identifiable, continuing particulars are central to any possible conceptual scheme. This means that any way of thinking which could, logically, be adopted must involve thought about objects of an external world. So a sceptic could not claim that the right, minimally ambitious, way of thinking about experience made no assumptions about the existence of such objects, for the answer would be that there cannot exist such a minimally ambitious way of thinking. In short, the tradition which would connect objectivity with the logical possibility of thinking at all stands in the way of straightforward contraposition of the argument that the rationality of supposing experience to be of objects entails the rationality of certain predictions of future existence.

To return then to the argument of p. 162. The alternative way of deriving something interesting from (1), (2) and (3) is to draw the rationality of some predictions of existence from (1), and then use (2) and (3) to give the further result that not only will some predictions of existence be justifiable, but also some other predictions from a class whose general truth is assured by the stability entailed by that continued existence.

The last chapter connected one way of reasoning inductively with general success. This chapter connects one way of reasoning inductively with general success in any world in which it would be possible to find ourselves. I said a little about the way in which the reasoning I identified in the last chapter expands to take in diversity and richness of evidence about the world in which we find ourselves. But we can only ensure general success for fractional extrapolations of regularities, and in this chapter, we only derive the rationality of expectations sanctioned by a policy weak enough for the requirement of objectivity to ensure its general success. Some people may not find this sort of prediction very exciting. They may be sure that they have confidence in propositions covering all objects of all sorts under all conditions at all times, and about these we have nothing to say, although anyone using such a proposition as an intermediary in anticipating and manipulating his immediate experience may find his practice justified by us anyhow. Anybody who finds this insufficient may well try to say more. In any case, it is enough at present that we can be justifiably confident that in some respects, and for some time, the future will indeed be like the past.

Bibliographical index

I have used *B.J.P.S.* as an abbreviation for the *British Journal of the Philosophy of Science*.

Altham, J. J. "A Note on Goodman's Paradox", *B.J.P.S.*, 1969. 82

Anderson, A., and Belnap, N. "Tautological Entailments", *Philosophical Studies*, 1962. 56

Barker, S. "Comments on Salmon's Vindication of Induction", in *Current Issues in the Philosophy of Science*, ed. H. Feigl and G. Maxwell, Holt, Rinehart & Winston, New York 1961. 95

Barker, S. and Achinstein, P. "On the New Riddle of Induction", *Philosophical Review*, 1960.

Bennett, J. *Kant's Analytic*, Cambridge University Press, Cambridge 1966. 161

Bernoulli, J. *Ars Conjectandi*, Basle 1713. 121

Black, M. *Problems of Analysis*, Routledge & Kegan Paul, London 1954. 155

Blackburn, S. "Moral Realism", in *Morality and Moral Reasoning*, ed. J. Casey, Methuen, London 1971. 24, 107.

"Goodman's Paradox", in *Studies in the Philosophy of Science*, American Philosophical Quarterly Monograph No. 3, ed. N. Rescher, Blackwell, Oxford 1969. 75

Braithwaite, R. B. *Scientific Explanation*, Cambridge University Press, Cambridge 1960. 155

Brody, B. A. "Confirmation and Explanation", *Journal of Philosophy*, 1968. 55

Bronowski, J. "The Scandal of Philosophy", *B.J.P.S.*, 1957. 137, 141

Carnap, R. *The Logical Foundations of Probability*, Routledge & Kegan Paul, London 1950. 53

The Continuum of Inductive Methods, University of Chicago Press, Chicago 1952. 48

Chisholm, R. *Perceiving*, Cornell University Press, Ithaca, N.Y. 1957. 23

Cohen, L. J. *The Implications of Induction*, Methuen, London 1970. 28

Edwards, P. "Bertrand Russell's Doubts about Induction", in *Logic and Language*, First Series, ed. A. Flew, Blackwell, Oxford 1951. 11–22

The Logic of Moral Discourse, The Free Press, New York 1955. 24

Feigl, H. "De Principiis non Disputandum...?", in *Philosophical*

Analysis, ed. M. Black, Prentice Hall, Englewood Cliffs, N.J. 1950. 93

Feigl, H. and Maxwell, G., eds. *Current Issues in the Philosophy of Science*, Holt, Rinehart & Winston, New York 1961. 95

Finetti, B. de. "Foresight: Its Logical Laws, its Subjective Sources", transl. in *Studies in Subjective Probability*, ed. H. Kyburg and H. Smokler, Wylie, New York 1964. 100

Goodman, N. *Fact, Fiction, and Forecast*, 2nd edn, Bobbs-Merrill Co. Inc., New York 1965 (1st edn, London 1955). 61–96

Hacking, I. *The Logic of Statistical Inference*, Cambridge University Press, Cambridge 1965. 53, 128

Harrod, R. *Foundations of Inductive Logic*, Macmillan, London 1956. 137–45

"The New Argument for Induction: Reply to Professor Popper", *B.J.P.S.*, 1959. 138

Hempel, C. "Studies in the Logic of Confirmation", *Mind*, 1945. 49

Hume, D. *A Treatise of Human Nature*, ed. L. A. Selby-Bigge, Clarendon Press, Oxford 1888. 44, 88

Abstract of a Treatise of Human Nature, Cambridge University Press, Cambridge 1938. 44, 88

Keynes, J. M. *A Treatise on Probability*, Macmillan, London 1921. 38, 98, 123–4

Kneale, W. *Probability and Induction*, Clarendon Press, Oxford 1949. 83, 93, 95, 116–21

Kyburg, H. "Recent Work in Inductive Logic", *American Philosophical Quarterly*, 1964. 86, 137, 138, 140

Kyburg, H. and Nagel, E. *Induction: Some Current Issues*, Wesleyan University Press, Middletown, Connecticut 1963. 95

Lewy, C. "G. E. Moore and the Naturalistic Fallacy", in *Studies in the Philosophy of Thought and Action*, ed. P. F. Strawson, Oxford University Press, London 1968. 26

Lucas, J. R. *The Concept of Probability*, Clarendon Press, Oxford 1970. 100

Nelson, E. J. "Intensional Relations", *Mind*, 1930. 56

Popper, K. R. *The Logic of Scientific Discovery*, Hutchinson, London 1968. 36, 87–92

"Mr. Harrod on Induction", *B.J.P.S.*, 1958. 137, 139

Putnam, H. " 'Degree of Confirmation' and Inductive Logic", in *The Philosophy of Rudolph Carnap*, ed. P. Schilpp, Open Court, Evanston, Ill. 1964. 48

Ramsey, F. P. "Truth and Probability", *The Foundations of Mathematics*, Routledge & Kegan Paul, London 1931. 100

Rescher, N. "Plausible Implication", *Analysis*, 1961. 52

Russell, B. *The Problems of Philosophy*, Oxford University Press, London 1962 (1st edn, 1912). 12, 112

Salmon, W. "Regular Rules of Induction", *Philosophical Review*, 1956. 93
  "On Vindicating Induction", in *Induction: Some Current Issues*, ed. H. Kyburg and E. Nagel, Wesleyan University Press, Middletown, Connecticut 1963. 95

Shoemaker, S. *Self-Knowledge and Self-Identity*, Cornell University Press, Ithaca, N.Y. 1963. 154

Strawson, P. F. *Introduction to Logical Theory*, Methuen, London 1963. 9, 16–20
  Individuals, Methuen, London 1959. 161

Todd, W. "Probability and the Theory of Confirmation", *Mind*, 1967. 58

Toulmin, S. "Probability", in *Essays in Conceptual Analysis*, ed. A. Flew, Macmillan, London 1963. 100, 102, 107

Urmson, J. O. "Some Questions Concerning Validity", in *Essays in Conceptual Analysis*, ed. A. Flew, Macmillan, London 1963. 23, 25
  The Emotive Theory of Ethics, Hutchinson University Library, London 1968. 17

Vincent, R. H. "The Paradox of Ideal Evidence", *Philosophical Review*, 1962. 36

Von Wright, G. H. *The Logical Problem of Induction*, Blackwell, Oxford 1957. 7

Wittgenstein, L. *Tractatus Logico-Philosophicus*, Routledge & Kegan Paul, London 1961. 159
  Philosophical Investigations, Blackwell, Oxford 1953. 78, 79